FOREWORD

The collection of "Everything Will Be Okay" travel phrasebooks published by T&P Books is designed for people traveling abroad for tourism and business. The phrasebooks contain what matters most - the essentials for basic communication. This is an indispensable set of phrases to "survive" while abroad.

This phrasebook will help you in most cases where you need to ask something, get directions, find out how much something costs, etc. It can also resolve difficult communication situations where gestures just won't help.

This book contains a lot of phrases that have been grouped according to the most relevant topics. A separate section of the book also provides a small dictionary with more than 1,500 important and useful words.

Take "Everything Will Be Okay" phrasebook with you on the road and you'll have an irreplaceable traveling companion who will help you find your way out of any situation and teach you to not fear speaking with foreigners.

TABLE OF CONTENTS

T&P Books Publishing

Travel phrasebooks collection
«Everything Will Be Okay!»

T&P Books Publishing

PHRASEBOOK

— ITALIAN —

THE MOST IMPORTANT PHRASES

This phrasebook contains the most important phrases and questions for basic communication
Everything you need to survive overseas

By Andrey Taranov

T&P BOOKS

Phrasebook + 1500-word dictionary

English-Italian phrasebook & concise dictionary

By Andrey Taranov

The collection of "Everything Will Be Okay" travel phrasebooks published by T&P Books is designed for people traveling abroad for tourism and business. The phrasebooks contain what matters most - the essentials for basic communication. This is an indispensable set of phrases to "survive" while abroad.

Another section of the book also provides a small dictionary with more than 1,500 useful words arranged alphabetically. The dictionary includes a lot of gastronomic terms and will be helpful when ordering food at a restaurant or buying groceries at the store.

T&P Books Publishing
www.tpbooks.com

ISBN: 978-1-78492-438-6

This book is also available in E-book formats.
Please visit www.tpbooks.com or the major online bookstores.

PRONUNCIATION

T&P phonetic alphabet	Italian example	English example
[a]	casco ['kasko]	shorter than in ask
[e]	sfera ['sfera]	elm, medal
[i]	filo ['filo]	shorter than in feet
[o]	dolce ['doltʃe]	pod, John
[u]	siluro [si'luro]	book
[y]	würstel ['vyrstel]	fuel, tuna
[b]	busta ['busta]	baby, book
[d]	andare [an'dare]	day, doctor
[ʣ]	zinco ['ʣinko]	beads, kids
[ʤ]	Norvegia [nor'veʤa]	joke, general
[ʒ]	garage [ga'raʒ]	forge, pleasure
[f]	ferrovia [ferro'via]	face, food
[g]	ago ['ago]	game, gold
[k]	cocktail ['koktejl]	clock, kiss
[j]	piazza ['pjattsa]	yes, New York
[l]	olive [o'live]	lace, people
[ʎ]	figlio ['fiʎʎo]	daily, million
[m]	mosaico [mo'zaiko]	magic, milk
[n]	treno ['treno]	name, normal
[ŋ]	granchio ['graŋkio]	English, ring
[ɲ]	magnete [ma'ɲete]	canyon, new
[p]	pallone [pal'lone]	pencil, private
[r]	futuro [fu'turo]	rice, radio
[s]	triste ['triste]	city, boss
[ʃ]	piscina [pi'ʃina]	machine, shark
[t]	estintore [estin'tore]	tourist, trip
[ts]	spezie ['spetsie]	cats, tsetse fly
[tʃ]	lancia ['lantʃa]	church, French
[v]	volo ['volo]	very, river
[w]	whisky ['wiski]	vase, winter
[z]	deserto [de'zerto]	zebra, please

LIST OF ABBREVIATIONS

English abbreviations

ab.	-	about
adj	-	adjective
adv	-	adverb
anim.	-	animate
as adj	-	attributive noun used as adjective
e.g.	-	for example
etc.	-	et cetera
fam.	-	familiar
fem.	-	feminine
form.	-	formal
inanim.	-	inanimate
masc.	-	masculine
math	-	mathematics
mil.	-	military
n	-	noun
pl	-	plural
pron.	-	pronoun
sb	-	somebody
sing.	-	singular
sth	-	something
v aux	-	auxiliary verb
vi	-	intransitive verb
vi, vt	-	intransitive, transitive verb
vt	-	transitive verb

Italian abbreviations

agg	-	adjective
f	-	feminine noun
f pl	-	feminine plural
m	-	masculine noun
m pl	-	masculine plural
m, f	-	masculine, feminine
pl	-	plural
v aus	-	auxiliary verb
vi	-	intransitive verb

vi, vt	-	intransitive, transitive verb
vr	-	reflexive verb
vt	-	transitive verb

T&P BOOKS

ITALIAN PHRASEBOOK

This section contains important phrases that may come in handy in various real-life situations.
The phrasebook will help you ask for directions, clarify a price, buy tickets, and order food at a restaurant

T&P Books Publishing

PHRASEBOOK
CONTENTS

T&P Books Publishing

Excuse me, ...	**Mi scusi, ...** [mi 'skuzi, ...]
Hello.	**Buongiorno.** [buon'dʒorno]
Thank you.	**Grazie.** [gratsie]
Good bye.	**Arrivederci.** [arrive'dertʃi]
Yes.	**Sì.** [si]
No.	**No.** [no]
I don't know.	**Non lo so.** [non lo so]
Where? | Where to? | When?	**Dove? | Dove? | Quando?** [dove? | 'dove? | 'kwando?]
I need ...	**Ho bisogno di ...** [o bi'zoɲo di ...]
I want ...	**Voglio ...** [voʎʎo ...]
Do you have ...?	**Avete ...?** [a'vete ...?]
Is there a ... here?	**C'è un /una/ ... qui?** [tʃe un /'una/ ... kwi?]
May I ...?	**Posso ...?** [posso ...?]
..., please (polite request)	**per favore** [per fa'vore]
I'm looking for ...	**Sto cercando ...** [sto tʃer'kando ...]
the restroom	**bagno** [baɲo]
an ATM	**bancomat** [bankomat]
a pharmacy (drugstore)	**farmacia** [farma'tʃija]
a hospital	**ospedale** [ospe'dale]
the police station	**stazione di polizia** [sta'tsjone di poli'tsia]
the subway	**metropolitana** [metropoli'tana]

a taxi	**taxi** ['taksi]
the train station	**stazione** [sta'tsjone]

My name is ...	**Mi chiamo ...** [mi 'kjamo ...]
What's your name?	**Come si chiama?** [kome si 'kjama?]
Could you please help me?	**Mi può aiutare, per favore?** [mi pu'o aju'tare, per fa'vore?]
I've got a problem.	**Ho un problema.** [o un pro'blema]
I don't feel well.	**Mi sento male.** [mi 'sento 'male]
Call an ambulance!	**Chiamate l'ambulanza!** [kja'mate lambu'lantsa!]
May I make a call?	**Posso fare una telefonata?** [posso 'fare 'una telefo'nata?]

I'm sorry.	**Mi dispiace.** [mi dis'pjatʃe]
You're welcome.	**Prego.** [prego]

I, me	**io** [io]
you (inform.)	**tu** [tu]
he	**lui** [lui]
she	**lei** ['lei]
they (masc.)	**loro** [loro]
they (fem.)	**loro** [loro]
we	**noi** [noi]
you (pl)	**voi** [voi]
you (sg, form.)	**Lei** ['lei]

ENTRANCE	**ENTRATA** [en'trata]
EXIT	**USCITA** [u'ʃita]
OUT OF ORDER	**FUORI SERVIZIO** [fu'ori ser'vitsio]
CLOSED	**CHIUSO** [kjuzo]

OPEN	**APERTO**
	[a'perto]
FOR WOMEN	**DONNE**
	[donne]
FOR MEN	**UOMINI**
	[u'omini]

Questions

Where? | **Dove?**
[dove?]

Where to? | **Dove?**
[dove?]

Where from? | **Da dove?**
[da 'dove?]

Why? | **Perché?**
[per'ke?]

For what reason? | **Perché?**
[per'ke?]

When? | **Quando?**
[kwando?]

How long? | **Per quanto tempo?**
[per 'kwanto 'tempo?]

At what time? | **A che ora?**
[a ke 'ora?]

How much? | **Quanto?**
[kwanto?]

Do you have ...? | **Avete ...?**
[a'vete ...?]

Where is ...? | **Dov'è ...?**
[dov'e ...?]

What time is it? | **Che ore sono?**
[ke 'ore 'sono?]

May I make a call? | **Posso fare una telefonata?**
[posso 'fare 'una telefo'nata?]

Who's there? | **Chi è?**
[ki 'e?]

Can I smoke here? | **Si può fumare qui?**
[si pu'o fu'mare kwi?]

May I ...? | **Posso ...?**
[posso ...?]

Needs

I'd like ...	**Vorrei ...** [vor'rej ...]
I don't want ...	**Non voglio ...** [non 'voʎʎo ...]
I'm thirsty.	**Ho sete.** [o 'sete]
I want to sleep.	**Ho sonno.** [o 'sonno]
I want ...	**Voglio ...** [voʎʎo ...]
to wash up	**lavarmi** [la'varmi]
to brush my teeth	**lavare i denti** [la'vare i 'denti]
to rest a while	**riposae un po'** [ripo'zae un 'po]
to change my clothes	**cambiare i vestiti** [kam'bjare i ve'stiti]
to go back to the hotel	**tornare in albergo** [tor'nare in al'bergo]
to buy ...	**comprare ...** [kom'prare ...]
to go to ...	**andare a ...** [an'dare a ...]
to visit ...	**visitare ...** [vizi'tare ...]
to meet with ...	**incontrare ...** [inkon'trare ...]
to make a call	**fare una telefonata** [fare 'una telefo'nata]
I'm tired.	**Sono stanco /stanca/.** [sono 'stanko /'stanka/]
We are tired.	**Siamo stanchi.** [sjamo 'staŋki]
I'm cold.	**Ho freddo.** [o 'freddo]
I'm hot.	**Ho caldo.** [o 'kaldo]
I'm OK.	**Sto bene.** [sto 'bene]

I need to make a call.

Devo fare una telefonata.
[devo 'fare 'una telefo'nata]

I need to go to the restroom.

Devo andare in bagno.
[devo an'dare in 'baɲo]

I have to go.

Devo andare.
[devo an'dare]

I have to go now.

Devo andare adesso.
[devo an'dare a'desso]

Asking for directions

Excuse me, ...	**Mi scusi, ...** [mi 'skuzi, ...]
Where is ...?	**Dove si trova ...?** [dove si 'trova ...?]
Which way is ...?	**Da che parte è ...?** [da ke 'parte e ...?]
Could you help me, please?	**Mi può aiutare, per favore?** [mi pu'o aju'tare, per fa'vore?]
I'm looking for ...	**Sto cercando ...** [sto tʃer'kando ...]
I'm looking for the exit.	**Sto cercando l'uscita.** [sto tʃer'kando lu'ʃita]
I'm going to ...	**Sto andando a ...** [sto an'dando a ...]
Am I going the right way to ...?	**Sto andando nella direzione giusta per ...?** [sto an'dando 'nella dire'tsjone 'dʒusta per ...?]
Is it far?	**E' lontano?** [e lon'tano?]
Can I get there on foot?	**Posso andarci a piedi?** [posso an'darsi a 'pjedi?]
Can you show me on the map?	**Può mostrarmi sulla piantina?** [pu'o mo'strarmi 'sulla pjan'tina?]
Show me where we are right now.	**Può mostrarmi dove ci troviamo?** [puo mo'strarmi 'dove tʃi tro'vjamo]
Here	**Qui** [kwi]
There	**Là** [la]
This way	**Da questa parte** [da 'kwesto 'parte]
Turn right.	**Giri a destra.** [dʒiri a 'destra]
Turn left.	**Giri a sinistra.** ['dʒiri a si'nistra]

first (second, third) turn

La prima (la seconda, la terza) strada
[la 'prima (la se'konda, la 'tertsa) 'strada]

to the right

a destra
[a 'destra]

to the left

a sinistra
[a si'nistra]

Go straight ahead.

Vada sempre dritto.
[vada 'sempre 'dritto]

Signs

WELCOME!	**BENVENUTO!** [benve'nuto!]
ENTRANCE	**ENTRATA** [en'trata]
EXIT	**USCITA** [u'ʃita]
PUSH	**SPINGERE** [spindʒere]
PULL	**TIRARE** [ti'rare]
OPEN	**APERTO** [a'perto]
CLOSED	**CHIUSO** [kjuzo]
FOR WOMEN	**DONNE** [donne]
FOR MEN	**UOMINI** [u'omini]
GENTLEMEN, GENTS	**BAGNO UOMINI** [baɲo u'omini]
WOMEN	**BAGNO DONNE** [baɲo 'donne]
DISCOUNTS	**SCONTI** [skonti]
SALE	**IN SALDO** [saldi]
FREE	**GRATIS** ['gratis]
NEW!	**NOVITÀ!** [novi'ta!]
ATTENTION!	**ATTENZIONE!** [atten'tsjone!]
NO VACANCIES	**COMPLETO** [kom'pleto]
RESERVED	**RISERVATO** [rizer'vato]
ADMINISTRATION	**AMMINISTRAZIONE** [amministra'tsjone]
STAFF ONLY	**RISERVATO AL PERSONALE** [rizer'vato al perso'nale]

BEWARE OF THE DOG! **ATTENTI AL CANE!**
[at'tenti al 'kane]

NO SMOKING! **VIETATO FUMARE**
[vje'tato fu'mare]

DO NOT TOUCH! **NON TOCCARE**
[non tok'kare]

DANGEROUS **PERICOLOSO**
[periko'lozo]

DANGER **PERICOLO**
[pe'rikolo]

HIGH VOLTAGE **ALTA TENSIONE**
[alta ten'sjone]

NO SWIMMING! **DIVIETO DI BALNEAZIONE**
[di'vjeto di balnea'tsjone]

OUT OF ORDER **FUORI SERVIZIO**
[fu'ori ser'vitsio]

FLAMMABLE **INFIAMMABILE**
[infjam'mabile]

FORBIDDEN **VIETATO**
[vje'tato]

NO TRESPASSING! **VIETATO L'ACCESSO**
[vje'tato la'tʃesso]

WET PAINT **PITTURA FRESCA**
[pitt'ura 'freska]

CLOSED FOR RENOVATIONS **CHIUSO PER RESTAURO**
[kjuzo per res'tauro]

WORKS AHEAD **LAVORI IN CORSO**
[la'vori in 'korso]

DETOUR **DEVIAZIONE**
[devia'tsjone]

Transportation. General phrases

plane	**aereo** [a'ereo]
train	**treno** [treno]
bus	**autobus** [autobus]
ferry	**traghetto** [tra'getto]
taxi	**taxi** ['taksi]
car	**macchina** ['makkina]
schedule	**orario** [o'rario]
Where can I see the schedule?	**Dove posso vedere l'orario?** [dove 'posso ve'dere lo'rario?]
workdays (weekdays)	**giorni feriali** [dʒorni fe'rjali]
weekends	**sabato e domenica** [sabato e do'menika]
holidays	**giorni festivi** [dʒorni fe'stivi]
DEPARTURE	**PARTENZA** [par'tentsa]
ARRIVAL	**ARRIVO** [ar'rivo]
DELAYED	**IN RITARDO** [in ri'tardo]
CANCELLED	**CANCELLATO** [kantʃelllato]
next (train, etc.)	**il prossimo** [il 'prossimo]
first	**il primo** [il 'primo]
last	**l'ultimo** [lultimo]
When is the next ...?	**Quando è il prossimo ...?** [kwando e il 'prossimo ...?]
When is the first ...?	**Quando è il primo ...?** [kwando e il 'primo ...?]

When is the last …?

Quando è l'ultimo …?
[kwando e 'lultimo …?]

transfer (change of trains, etc.)

scalo
[skalo]

to make a transfer

effettuare uno scalo
[efettu'are 'uno 'skalo]

Do I need to make a transfer?

Devo cambiare?
[devo kam'bjare?]

Buying tickets

Where can I buy tickets?	**Dove posso comprare i biglietti?** [dove 'posso kom'prare i biʎ'ʎeti?]
ticket	**biglietto** [biʎ'ʎetto]
to buy a ticket	**comprare un biglietto** [kom'prare un biʎ'ʎetto]
ticket price	**il prezzo del biglietto** [il 'prettso del biʎ'ʎetto]

Where to?	**Dove?** [dove?]
To what station?	**In quale stazione?** [in 'kwale sta'tsjone?]
I need ...	**Avrei bisogno di ...** [av'rej bi'zoɲo di ...]
one ticket	**un biglietto** [un biʎ'ʎetto]
two tickets	**due biglietti** [due biʎ'ʎeti]
three tickets	**tre biglietti** [tre biʎ'ʎeti]

one-way	**solo andata** [solo an'data]
round-trip	**andata e ritorno** [an'data e ri'torno]
first class	**prima classe** [prima 'klasse]
second class	**seconda classe** [se'konda 'klasse]

today	**oggi** [odʒi]
tomorrow	**domani** [do'mani]
the day after tomorrow	**dopodomani** [dopodo'mani]
in the morning	**la mattina** [la mat'tina]
in the afternoon	**nel pomeriggio** [nel pome'ridʒo]
in the evening	**la sera** [la 'sera]

aisle seat

posto lato corridoio
[posto 'lato korri'dojo]

window seat

posto lato finestrino
[posto 'lato fine'strino]

How much?

Quanto?
[kwanto?]

Can I pay by credit card?

Posso pagare con la carta di credito?
[posso pa'gare kon la 'karta di 'kredito?]

Bus

bus	**autobus** [autobus]
intercity bus	**autobus interurbano** [autobus interur'bano]
bus stop	**fermata dell'autobus** [fer'mata dell 'autobus]
Where's the nearest bus stop?	**Dov'è la fermata dell'autobus più vicina?** [dov'e la fer'mata dell 'autobus pju vi'tʃina?]
number (bus ~, etc.)	**numero** [numero]
Which bus do I take to get to ...?	**Quale autobus devo prendere per andare a ...?** [kwale 'autobus 'devo 'prendere per an'dare a ...?]
Does this bus go to ...?	**Questo autobus va a ...?** [kwesto 'autobus va a ...?]
How frequent are the buses?	**Qual'è la frequenza delle corse degli autobus?** [kwal e la fre'kwentsa 'delle 'korse 'deʎʎi 'autobus?]

every 15 minutes	**ogni quindici minuti** [oɲi 'kwinditʃi mi'nuti]
every half hour	**ogni mezzora** [oɲi med'dzora]
every hour	**ogni ora** [oɲi 'ora]
several times a day	**più a volte al giorno** [pju a 'volte al 'dʒorno]
... times a day	**... volte al giorno** [... 'volte al 'dʒorno]

schedule	**orario** [o'rario]
Where can I see the schedule?	**Dove posso vedere l'orario?** [dove 'posso ve'dere lo'rario?]
When is the next bus?	**Quando passa il prossimo autobus?** [kwando 'passa il 'prossimo 'autobus?]
When is the first bus?	**A che ora è il primo autobus?** [a ke 'ora e il 'primo 'autobus?]
When is the last bus?	**A che ora è l'ultimo autobus?** [a ke 'ora e 'lultimo 'autobus?]

stop

fermata
[fer'mata]

next stop

prossima fermata
[prossima fer'mata]

last stop (terminus)

ultima fermata
[ultima fer'mata]

Stop here, please.

Può fermarsi qui, per favore.
[pu'o fer'marsi kwi, per fa'vore]

Excuse me, this is my stop.

Mi scusi, questa è la mia fermata.
[mi 'skuzi, 'kwesta e la 'mia fer'mata]

Train

train	**treno** [treno]
suburban train	**treno locale** [treno lo'kale]
long-distance train	**treno a lunga percorrenza** [treno a 'lunga perkor'rentsa]
train station	**stazione** [sta'tsjone]
Excuse me, where is the exit to the platform?	**Mi scusi, dov'è l'uscita per il binario?** [mi 'skuzi, dov'e lu'ʃita per il binario?]
Does this train go to …?	**Questo treno va a …?** [kwesto 'treno va a …?]
next train	**il prossimo treno** [il 'prossimo 'treno]
When is the next train?	**Quando è il prossimo treno?** [kwando e il 'prossimo 'treno?]
Where can I see the schedule?	**Dove posso vedere l'orario?** [dove 'posso ve'dere lo'rario?]
From which platform?	**Da quale binario?** [da 'kwale bi'nario?]
When does the train arrive in …?	**Quando il treno arriva a … ?** [kwando il 'treno ar'riva a …?]
Please help me.	**Mi può aiutare, per favore.** [mi pu'o aju'tare, per fa'vore]
I'm looking for my seat.	**Sto cercando il mio posto.** [sto tʃer'kando il 'mio 'posto]
We're looking for our seats.	**Stiamo cercando i nostri posti.** [stjamo tʃer'kando i 'nostri 'posti]
My seat is taken.	**Il mio posto è occupato.** [il 'mio 'posto e okku'pato]
Our seats are taken.	**I nostri posti sono occupati.** [i 'nostri 'posti 'sono okku'pati]
I'm sorry but this is my seat.	**Mi scusi, ma questo è il mio posto.** [mi 'skwzi, ma 'kwesto e il 'mio 'posto]
Is this seat taken?	**E' occupato?** [e okku'pato?]
May I sit here?	**Posso sedermi qui?** [posso se'dermi kwi?]

On the train. Dialogue (No ticket)

Ticket, please.

Biglietto per favore.
[biʎ'ʎetto per fa'vore]

I don't have a ticket.

Non ho il biglietto.
[non 'o il biʎ'ʎetto]

I lost my ticket.

Ho perso il biglietto.
[o 'perso il biʎ'ʎetto]

I forgot my ticket at home.

Ho dimenticato il biglietto a casa.
[o dimenti'kato il biʎ'ʎetto a 'kaza]

You can buy a ticket from me.

Può acquistare il biglietto da me.
[pu'o akwi'stare il biʎ'ʎetto da 'me]

You will also have to pay a fine.

Deve anche pagare una multa.
[deve 'aŋke pa'gare 'una 'multa]

Okay.

Va bene.
[va 'bene]

Where are you going?

Dove va?
[dove va?]

I'm going to …

Vado a …
[vado a …]

How much? I don't understand.

Quanto? Non capisco.
[kwanto? non ka'pisko]

Write it down, please.

Lo può scrivere, per favore?
[lo pu'o 'skrivere, per fa'vore]

Okay. Can I pay with a credit card?

D'accordo. Posso pagare con la carta di credito?
[dak'kordo. 'posso pa'gare kon la 'karta di 'kredito?]

Yes, you can.

Sì.
[si]

Here's your receipt.

Ecco la sua ricevuta.
[ekko la 'sua ritʃe'vuta]

Sorry about the fine.

Mi dispiace per la multa.
[mi dis'pjatʃe per la 'multa]

That's okay. It was my fault.

Va bene così. È stata colpa mia.
[va 'bene ko'si. e 'stata 'kolpa 'mia]

Enjoy your trip.

Buon viaggio.
[bu'on 'vjadʒo]

Taxi

taxi	**taxi** ['taksi]
taxi driver	**tassista** [tas'sista]
to catch a taxi	**prendere un taxi** [prendere un 'taksi]
taxi stand	**posteggio taxi** [pos'tedʒo 'taksi]
Where can I get a taxi?	**Dove posso prendere un taxi?** [dove 'posso 'prendere un 'taksi?]

to call a taxi	**chiamare un taxi** [kja'mare un 'taksi]
I need a taxi.	**Ho bisogno di un taxi.** [o bi'zoɲo di un 'taksi]
Right now.	**Adesso.** [a'desso]
What is your address (location)?	**Qual'è il suo indirizzo?** [kwal e il 'suo indi'rittso?]
My address is ...	**Il mio indirizzo è ...** [il 'mio indi'rittso e ...]
Your destination?	**La sua destinazione?** [la 'sua destina'tsjone?]
Excuse me, ...	**Mi scusi, ...** [mi 'skuzi, ...]
Are you available?	**E' libero?** [e 'libero?]
How much is it to get to ...?	**Quanto costa andare a ...?** [kwanto 'kosta an'dare a ...?]
Do you know where it is?	**Sapete dove si trova?** [sa'pete 'dove si 'trova?]

Airport, please.	**All'aeroporto, per favore.** [all aero'porto, per fa'vore]
Stop here, please.	**Si fermi qui, per favore.** [si 'fermi kwi, per fa'vore]
It's not here.	**Non è qui.** [non e kwi]
This is the wrong address.	**È l'indirizzo sbagliato.** [e lindi'rittso zbaʎ'ʎato]
Turn left.	**Giri a sinistra.** [dʒiri a si'nistra]
Turn right.	**Giri a destra.** [dʒiri a 'destra]

How much do I owe you?

Quanto le devo?
[kwanto le 'devo?]

I'd like a receipt, please.

Potrei avere una ricevuta, per favore.
[po'trej a'vere 'una ritʃe'vuta, per fa'vore]

Keep the change.

Tenga il resto.
[tenga il 'resto]

Would you please wait for me?

Può aspettarmi, per favore?
[pu'o aspe'tarmi, per fa'vore?]

five minutes

cinque minuti
[tʃinkwe mi'nuti]

ten minutes

dieci minuti
['djetʃi mi'nuti]

fifteen minutes

quindici minuti
[kwinditʃi mi'nuti]

twenty minutes

venti minuti
[venti mi'nuti]

half an hour

mezzora
[med'dzora]

Hotel

Hello.	**Salve.** [salve]
My name is ...	**Mi chiamo ...** [mi 'kjamo ...]
I have a reservation.	**Ho prenotato una camera.** [o preno'tato 'una 'kamera]
I need ...	**Ho bisogno di ...** [o bi'zoɲo di ...]
a single room	**una camera singola** [una 'kamera 'singola]
a double room	**una camera doppia** [una 'kamera 'doppia]
How much is that?	**Quanto costa questo?** [kwanto 'kosta 'kwesto?]
That's a bit expensive.	**È un po' caro.** [e un 'po 'karo]
Do you have anything else?	**Avete qualcos'altro?** [a'vete kwal'koz 'altro?]
I'll take it.	**La prendo.** [la 'prendo]
I'll pay in cash.	**Pago in contanti.** [pago in kon'tanti]
I've got a problem.	**Ho un problema.** [o un pro'blema]
My ... is broken.	**Il mio ... è rotto /La mia ... è rotta/** [il 'mio ... e 'rotto /la 'mia ... e 'rotta/]
My ... is out of order.	**Il mio /La mia/ ... è fuori servizio.** [il 'mio /la 'mia/ ... e fu'ori ser'vitsio]
TV	**televisore** [televi'zore]
air conditioner	**condizionatore** [konditsiona'tore]
tap	**rubinetto** [rubi'netto]
shower	**doccia** [dotʃa]
sink	**lavandino** [lavan'dino]
safe	**cassa forte** [kassa 'forte]

door lock	**serratura** [serra'tura]
electrical outlet	**presa elettrica** [preza e'lettrika]
hairdryer	**asciugacapelli** [aʃuga·ka'pelli]

I don't have ...	**Non ho ...** [non o ...]
water	**l'acqua** [lakwa]
light	**la luce** [la 'lutʃe]
electricity	**l'elettricità** [leletritʃi'ta]

Can you give me ...?	**Può darmi ...?** [pu'o 'darmi ...?]
a towel	**un asciugamano** [un aʃuga'mano]
a blanket	**una coperta** [una ko'perta]
slippers	**delle pantofole** [delle pan'tofole]
a robe	**un accappatoio** [un akkappa'tojo]
shampoo	**dello shampoo** [dello 'ʃampo]
soap	**del sapone** [del sa'pone]

I'd like to change rooms.	**Vorrei cambiare la camera.** [vor'rej kam'bjare la 'kamera]
I can't find my key.	**Non trovo la chiave.** [non 'trovo la 'kjave]
Could you open my room, please?	**Potrebbe aprire la mia camera, per favore?** [po'trebbe a'prire la mia 'kamera, per fa'vore?]
Who's there?	**Chi è?** [ki 'e?]
Come in!	**Avanti!** [a'vanti!]
Just a minute!	**Un attimo!** [un 'attimo!]

Not right now, please.	**Non adesso, per favore.** [non a'desso, per fa'vore]
Come to my room, please.	**Può venire nella mia camera, per favore.** [pu'o ve'nire 'nella 'mia 'kamera, per fa'vore]

I'd like to order food service.	**Vorrei ordinare qualcosa da mangiare.** [vor'rej ordi'nare kwal'koza da man'dʒare]
My room number is …	**Il mio numero di camera è …** [il 'mio 'numero di 'kamera e …]

I'm leaving …	**Parto …** [parto …]
We're leaving …	**Partiamo …** [par'tjamo …]
right now	**adesso** [a'desso]
this afternoon	**questo pomeriggio** [kwesto pome'ridʒo]
tonight	**stasera** [sta'sera]
tomorrow	**domani** [do'mani]
tomorrow morning	**domani mattina** [do'mani mat'tina]
tomorrow evening	**domani sera** [do'mani 'sera]
the day after tomorrow	**dopodomani** [dopodo'mani]

I'd like to pay.	**Vorrei pagare.** [vor'rej sal'dare il 'konto]
Everything was wonderful.	**È stato tutto magnifico.** [e 'stato 'tutto ma'ɲifiko]
Where can I get a taxi?	**Dove posso prendere un taxi?** [dove 'posso 'prendere un 'taksi?]
Would you call a taxi for me, please?	**Potrebbe chiamarmi un taxi, per favore?** [po'trebbe kja'marmi un 'taksi, per fa'vore?]

Restaurant

Can I look at the menu, please?

Posso vedere il menù, per favore?
[posso ve'dere il me'nu, per fa'vore?]

Table for one.

Un tavolo per una persona.
[un 'tavolo per 'uno per'sona]

There are two (three, four) of us.

Siamo in due (tre, quattro).
[sjamo in 'due (tre, 'kwattro)]

Smoking

Fumatori
[fuma'tori]

No smoking

Non fumatori
[non fuma'tori]

Excuse me! (addressing a waiter)

Mi scusi!
[mi 'skuzi!]

menu

il menù
[il me'nu]

wine list

la lista dei vini
[la 'lista 'dei 'vini]

The menu, please.

Posso avere il menù, per favore.
[posso a'vere il me'nu, per fa'vore]

Are you ready to order?

È pronto per ordinare?
[e 'pronto per ordi'nare?]

What will you have?

Cosa gradisce?
[koza gra'diʃe?]

I'll have …

Prendo …
[prendo …]

I'm a vegetarian.

Sono vegetariano /vegetariana/.
[sono vedʒeta'rjano /vedʒeta'rjana/]

meat

carne
[karne]

fish

pesce
[peʃe]

vegetables

verdure
[ver'dure]

Do you have vegetarian dishes?

Avete dei piatti vegetariani?
[a'vete 'dei 'pjatti vedʒeta'rjani?]

I don't eat pork.

Non mangio carne di maiale.
[non 'mandʒo 'karne di ma'jale]

Band-Aid

Lui /lei/ non mangia la carne.
[lui /'lei/ non 'mandʒa la 'karne]

I am allergic to …

Sono allergico a …
[sono al'lerdʒiko a …]

Would you please bring me ...

Potrebbe portarmi ...
[po'trebbe por'tarmi ...]

salt | pepper | sugar

del sale | del pepe | dello zucchero
[del 'sale | del 'pepe | 'dello 'tsukkero]

coffee | tea | dessert

un caffè | un tè | un dolce
[un ka'fe | un te | un 'doltʃe]

water | sparkling | plain

dell'acqua | frizzante | naturale
[dell 'akwa | frid'dzante | natu'rale]

a spoon | fork | knife

un cucchiaio | una forchetta | un coltello
[un kuk'kjajo | una for'ketta | un kol'tello]

a plate | napkin

un piatto | un tovagliolo
[un 'pjatto | un tovaʎ'ʎolo]

Enjoy your meal!

Buon appetito!
[bu'on appe'tito!]

One more, please.

Un altro, per favore.
[un 'altro, per fa'vore]

It was very delicious.

È stato squisito.
[e 'stato skwi'zito]

---

check | change | tip

il conto | il resto | la mancia
[il 'konto | il 'resto | la 'mantʃa]

Check, please.
(Could I have the check, please?)

Il conto, per favore.
[il 'konto, per fa'vore]

Can I pay by credit card?

Posso pagare con la carta di credito?
[posso pa'gare kon la 'karta di 'kredito?]

I'm sorry, there's a mistake here.

Mi scusi, c'è un errore.
[mi 'skuzi, tʃe un er'rore]

Shopping

Can I help you?	**Posso aiutarla?** [posso aju'tarla?]
Do you have ...?	**Avete ...?** [a'vete ...?]
I'm looking for ...	**Sto cercando ...** [sto tʃer'kando ...]
I need ...	**Ho bisogno di ...** [o bi'zoɲo di ...]

I'm just looking.	**Sto guardando.** [sto gwar'dando]
We're just looking.	**Stiamo guardando.** [stjamo gwar'dando]
I'll come back later.	**Ripasserò più tardi.** [ripasse'ro pju 'tardi]
We'll come back later.	**Ripasseremo più tardi.** [ripasse'remo pju 'tardi]
discounts	sale	**sconti	saldi** [skonti	'saldi]

Would you please show me ...	**Per favore, mi può far vedere ...?** [per fa'vore, mi pu'o far ve'dere ...?]
Would you please give me ...	**Per favore, potrebbe darmi ...** [per fa'vore, po'trebbe 'darmi ...]
Can I try it on?	**Posso provarlo?** [posso pro'varlo?]
Excuse me, where's the fitting room?	**Mi scusi, dov'è il camerino?** [mi 'skuzi, dov'e il kame'rino?]
Which color would you like?	**Che colore desidera?** [ke ko'lore de'zidera?]
size	length	**taglia	lunghezza** [taʎʎa	lun'gettsa]
How does it fit?	**Come le sta?** [kome le sta?]

How much is it?	**Quanto costa questo?** [kwanto 'kosta 'kwesto?]
That's too expensive.	**È troppo caro.** [e 'troppo 'karo]
I'll take it.	**Lo prendo.** [lo 'prendo]
Excuse me, where do I pay?	**Mi scusi, dov'è la cassa?** [mi 'skuzi, dov'e la 'kassa?]

Will you pay in cash or credit card?

Paga in contanti o con carta di credito?
[paga in kon'tanti o kon 'karta di 'kredito?]

In cash | with credit card

In contanti | con carta di credito
[in kon'tanti | kon 'karta di 'kredito]

Do you want the receipt?

Vuole lo scontrino?
[vu'ole lo skon'trino?]

Yes, please.

Sì, grazie.
[si, 'gratsie]

No, it's OK.

No, va bene così.
[no, va 'bene ko'zi]

Thank you. Have a nice day!

Grazie. Buona giornata!
[gratsie. bu'ona ʤor'nata!]

In town

Excuse me, ...
Mi scusi, per favore ...
[mi 'skuzi, per fa'vore ...]

I'm looking for ...
Sto cercando ...
[sto tʃer'kando ...]

the subway
la metropolitana
[la metropoli'tana]

my hotel
il mio albergo
[il 'mio al'bergo]

the movie theater
il cinema
[il 'tʃinema]

a taxi stand
il posteggio taxi
[il po'stedʒo 'taksi]

an ATM
un bancomat
[un 'bankomat]

a foreign exchange office
un ufficio dei cambi
[un uf'fitʃio 'dei 'kambi]

an internet café
un internet café
[un inter'net ka'fe]

... street
via ...
[via ...]

this place
questo posto
[kwesto 'posto]

Do you know where ... is?
Sa dove si trova ...?
[sa 'dove si 'trova ...?]

Which street is this?
Come si chiama questa via?
[kome si 'kjama 'kwesta 'via?]

Show me where we are right now.
Può mostrarmi dove ci troviamo?
[pu'o mo'strarmi 'dove tʃi tro'vjamo]

Can I get there on foot?
Posso andarci a piedi?
[posso an'dartʃi a 'pjedi?]

Do you have a map of the city?
Avete la piantina della città?
[a'vete la pjan'tina 'della tʃitta?]

How much is a ticket to get in?
Quanto costa un biglietto?
[kwanto 'kosta un biʎ'ʎetto?]

Can I take pictures here?
Si può fotografare?
[si pu'o fotogra'fare?]

Are you open?
E' aperto?
[e a'perto?]

When do you open?

Quando aprite?
[kwando a'prite?]

When do you close?

Quando chiudete?
[kwando kju'dete?]

Money

money	**Soldi** [soldi]
cash	**contanti** [kon'tanti]
paper money	**banconote** [banko'note]
loose change	**monete** [mo'nete]
check | change | tip	**conto | resto | mancia** [konto | 'resto | 'mantʃa]
credit card	**carta di credito** [karta di 'kredito]
wallet	**portafoglio** [porta·'foʎʎo]
to buy	**comprare** [kom'prare]
to pay	**pagare** [pa'gare]
fine	**multa** [multa]
free	**gratuito** [gratu'ito]
Where can I buy ...?	**Dove posso comprare ...?** [dove 'posso kom'prare ...?]
Is the bank open now?	**La banca è aperta adesso?** [la 'banka e a'perta a'desso?]
When does it open?	**Quando apre?** [kwando 'apre?]
When does it close?	**Quando chiude?** [kwando 'kjude?]
How much?	**Quanto costa?** [kwanto 'kosta?]
How much is this?	**Quanto costa questo?** [kwanto 'kosta 'kwesto?]
That's too expensive.	**È troppo caro.** [e 'troppo 'karo]
Excuse me, where do I pay?	**Scusi, dov'è la cassa?** [skuzi, dov'e la 'kassa?]
Check, please.	**Il conto, per favore.** [il 'konto, per fa'vore]

Can I pay by credit card?

Posso pagare con la carta di credito?
[posso pa'gare kon la 'karta di 'kredito?]

Is there an ATM here?

C'è un bancomat?
[tʃe un 'bankomat?]

I'm looking for an ATM.

Sto cercando un bancomat.
[sto tʃer'kando un 'bankomat]

I'm looking for a foreign exchange
office.

Sto cercando un ufficio dei cambi.
[sto tʃer'kando un uf'fitʃio dei 'kambi]

I'd like to change ...

Vorrei cambiare ...
[vor'rej kam'bjare ...]

What is the exchange rate?

Quanto è il tasso di cambio?
[kwanto e il 'tasso di 'kambio]

Do you need my passport?

Ha bisogno del mio passaporto?
[a bi'zoɲo del 'mio passa'porto?]

Time

What time is it?	**Che ore sono?** [ke 'ore 'sono?]
When?	**Quando?** [kwando?]
At what time?	**A che ora?** [a ke 'ora?]
now | later | after …	**adesso | più tardi | dopo …** [a'desso | pju 'tardi | 'dopo …]
one o'clock	**l'una** [luna]
one fifteen	**l'una e un quarto** [luna e un 'kwarto]
one thirty	**l'una e trenta** [luna e 'trenta]
one forty-five	**l'una e quarantacinque** [luna e kwa'ranta 'tʃinkwe]
one | two | three	**uno | due | tre** [uno | 'due | tre]
four | five | six	**quattro | cinque | sei** [kwattro | 'tʃinkwe | sej]
seven | eight | nine	**sette | otto | nove** [sette | 'otto | 'nove]
ten | eleven | twelve	**dieci | undici | dodici** [djetʃi | 'unditʃi | 'doditʃi]
in …	**fra …** [fra …]
five minutes	**cinque minuti** [tʃinkwe mi'nuti]
ten minutes	**dieci minuti** ['djetʃi mi'nuti]
fifteen minutes	**quindici minuti** [kwinditʃi mi'nuti]
twenty minutes	**venti minuti** [venti mi'nuti]
half an hour	**mezzora** [med'dzora]
an hour	**un'ora** [un 'ora]

in the morning	**la mattina**
	[la mat'tina]
early in the morning	**la mattina presto**
	[la mat'tina 'presto]
this morning	**questa mattina**
	[kwesta mat'tina]
tomorrow morning	**domani mattina**
	[do'mani mat'tina]

in the middle of the day	**all'ora di pranzo**
	[all 'ora di 'prantso]
in the afternoon	**nel pomeriggio**
	[nel pome'ridʒo]
in the evening	**la sera**
	[la 'sera]
tonight	**stasera**
	[sta'sera]

at night	**la notte**
	[la 'notte]
yesterday	**ieri**
	['jeri]
today	**oggi**
	[odʒi]
tomorrow	**domani**
	[do'mani]
the day after tomorrow	**dopodomani**
	[dopodo'mani]

What day is it today?	**Che giorno è oggi?**
	[ke 'dʒorno e 'odʒi?]
It's ...	**Oggi è ...**
	[odʒi e ...?]
Monday	**lunedì**
	[lune'di]
Tuesday	**martedì**
	[marte'di]
Wednesday	**mercoledì**
	[merkole'di]

Thursday	**giovedì**
	[dʒove'di]
Friday	**venerdì**
	[vener'di]
Saturday	**sabato**
	[sabato]
Sunday	**domenica**
	[do'menika]

Greetings. Introductions

Hello.	**Salve.** [salve]
Pleased to meet you.	**Lieto di conoscerla.** [leto di ko'noʃerla]
Me too.	**Il piacere è mio.** [il pja'tʃere e 'mio]
I'd like you to meet ...	**Vi presento ...** [vi pre'zento ...]
Nice to meet you.	**Molto piacere.** [molto pja'tʃere]

How are you?	**Come sta?** [kome sta?]
My name is ...	**Mi chiamo ...** [mi 'kjamo ...]
His name is ...	**Si chiama ...** [si 'kjama ...]
Her name is ...	**Si chiama ...** [si 'kjama ...]
What's your name?	**Come si chiama?** [kome si 'kjama?]
What's his name?	**Come si chiama lui?** [kome si 'kjama 'lui?]
What's her name?	**Come si chiama lei?** [kome si 'kjama 'lei?]

What's your last name?	**Qual'è il suo cognome?** [kwal e 'suo ko'ɲome?]
You can call me ...	**Può chiamarmi ...** [pu'o kja'marmi ...]
Where are you from?	**Da dove viene?** [da 'dove 'vjene?]
I'm from ...	**Vengo da ...** [vengo da ...]
What do you do for a living?	**Che lavoro fa?** [ke la'voro 'fa?]
Who is this?	**Chi è?** [ki 'e?]
Who is he?	**Chi è lui?** [ki e 'lui?]
Who is she?	**Chi è lei?** [ki e 'lei?]
Who are they?	**Chi sono loro?** [ki 'sono 'loro?]

This is … **Questo /Questa/ è …**
[kwesto /'kwesta/ e …]

my friend (masc.) **il mio amico**
[il 'mio a'miko]

my friend (fem.) **la mia amica**
[la 'mia a'mika]

my husband **mio marito**
[mio ma'rito]

my wife **mia moglie**
[mia 'moʎʎe]

my father **mio padre**
[mio 'padre]

my mother **mia madre**
[mia 'madre]

my brother **mio fratello**
[mio fra'tello]

my sister **mia sorella**
[mia so'rella]

my son **mio figlio**
[mio 'fiʎʎo]

my daughter **mia figlia**
[mia 'fiʎʎa]

This is our son. **Questo è nostro figlio.**
[kwesto e 'nostro 'fiʎʎo]

This is our daughter. **Questa è nostra figlia.**
[kwesta e 'nostra 'fiʎʎa]

These are my children. **Questi sono i miei figli.**
[kwesti 'sono i 'mjei 'fiʎʎi]

These are our children. **Questi sono i nostri figli.**
[kwesti 'sono i 'nostri 'fiʎʎi]

Farewells

Good bye!	**Arrivederci!** [arrive'dertʃi!]
Bye! (inform.)	**Ciao!** [tʃao!]
See you tomorrow.	**A domani.** [a do'mani]
See you soon.	**A presto.** [a 'presto]
See you at seven.	**Ci vediamo alle sette.** [tʃi ve'djamo 'alle 'sette]
Have fun!	**Divertitevi!** [diverti'tevi!]
Talk to you later.	**Ci sentiamo più tardi.** [tʃi sen'tjamo 'pju 'tardi]
Have a nice weekend.	**Buon fine settimana.** [bu'on 'fine setti'mana]
Good night.	**Buona notte** [bu'ona 'notte]
It's time for me to go.	**Adesso devo andare.** [a'desso 'devo an'dare]
I have to go.	**Devo andare.** [devo an'dare]
I will be right back.	**Torno subito.** [torno 'subito]
It's late.	**È tardi.** [e 'tardi]
I have to get up early.	**Domani devo alzarmi presto.** [do'mani 'devo al'tsarmi 'presto]
I'm leaving tomorrow.	**Parto domani.** [parto do'mani]
We're leaving tomorrow.	**Partiamo domani.** [par'tjamo do'mani]
Have a nice trip!	**Buon viaggio!** [bu'on 'vjadʒo!]
It was nice meeting you.	**È stato un piacere conoscerla.** [e 'stato un pja'tʃere di ko'noʃerla]
It was nice talking to you.	**È stato un piacere parlare con lei.** [e 'stato un pja'tʃere par'lare kon lej]
Thanks for everything.	**Grazie di tutto.** [gratsie di 'tutto]

I had a very good time.

Mi sono divertito.
[mi 'sono diver'tito]

We had a very good time.

Ci siamo divertiti.
[tʃi 'sjamo di'vertiti]

It was really great.

È stato straordinario.
[e 'stato straordi'nario]

I'm going to miss you.

Mi mancherà.
[mi maŋke'ra]

We're going to miss you.

Ci mancherà.
[tʃi maŋke'ra]

Good luck!

Buona fortuna!
[bu'ona for'tuna!]

Say hi to …

Mi saluti …
[mi sa'luti …]

Foreign language

I don't understand.	**Non capisco.** [non ka'pisko]
Write it down, please.	**Lo può scrivere, per favore?** [lo pu'o 'skrivere, per fa'vore]
Do you speak ...?	**Parla ...?** [parla ...?]
I speak a little bit of ...	**Parlo un po' ...** [parlo un po ...]
English	**inglese** [in'gleze]
Turkish	**turco** [turko]
Arabic	**arabo** [arabo]
French	**francese** [fran'tʃeze]
German	**tedesco** [te'desko]
Italian	**italiano** [ita'ljano]
Spanish	**spagnolo** [spa'ɲolo]
Portuguese	**portoghese** [porto'geze]
Chinese	**cinese** [tʃi'neze]
Japanese	**giapponese** [dʒappo'neze]
Can you repeat that, please.	**Può ripetere, per favore.** [pu'o ri'petere, per fa'vore]
I understand.	**Capisco.** [ka'pisko]
I don't understand.	**Non capisco.** [non ka'pisko]
Please speak more slowly.	**Può parlare più piano, per favore.** [pu'o par'lare pju 'pjano, per fa'vore]
Is that correct? (Am I saying it right?)	**È corretto?** [e kor'retto?]
What is this? (What does this mean?)	**Cos'è questo?** [koz e 'kwesto?]

49

Apologies

Excuse me, please.	**Mi scusi, per favore.** [mi 'skuzi, per fa'vore]
I'm sorry.	**Mi dispiace.** [mi dis'pjatʃe]
I'm really sorry.	**Mi dispiace molto.** [mi dis'pjatʃe 'molto]
Sorry, it's my fault.	**Mi dispiace, è colpa mia.** [mi dis'pjatʃe, e 'kolpa 'mia]
My mistake.	**È stato un mio errore.** [e 'stato un 'mio er'rore]
May I ...?	**Posso ...?** [posso ...?]
Do you mind if I ...?	**Le dispiace se ...?** [le dis'pjatʃe se ...?]
It's OK.	**Non fa niente.** [non fa 'njente]
It's all right.	**Tutto bene.** [tutto 'bene]
Don't worry about it.	**Non si preoccupi.** [non si pre'okkupi]

Agreement

Yes.	**Sì.** [si]
Yes, sure.	**Sì, certo.** [si, 'tʃerto]
OK (Good!)	**Bene.** [bene]
Very well.	**Molto bene.** [molto 'bene]
Certainly!	**Certamente!** [tʃerta'mente!]
I agree.	**Sono d'accordo.** [sono dak'kordo]
That's correct.	**Esatto.** [e'satto]
That's right.	**Giusto.** [dʒusto]
You're right.	**Ha ragione.** [a ra'dʒone]
I don't mind.	**È lo stesso.** [e lo 'stesso]
Absolutely right.	**È assolutamente corretto.** [e assoluta'mente kor'retto]
It's possible.	**È possibile.** [e pos'sibile]
That's a good idea.	**È una buona idea.** [e 'una bu'ona i'dea]
I can't say no.	**Non posso dire di no.** [non 'posso 'dire di no]
I'd be happy to.	**Ne sarei lieto.** [ne sa'rei 'leto]
With pleasure.	**Con piacere.** [kon pja'tʃere]

Refusal. Expressing doubt

No.
No.
[no]

Certainly not.
Sicuramente no.
[sikura'mente no]

I don't agree.
Non sono d'accordo.
[non 'sono dak'kordo]

I don't think so.
Non penso.
[non 'penso]

It's not true.
Non è vero.
[non e 'vero]

You are wrong.
Si sbaglia.
[si 'zbaʎʎa]

I think you are wrong.
Penso che lei si stia sbagliando.
[penso ke 'lei si stia zbaʎ'ʎando]

I'm not sure.
Non sono sicuro.
[non 'sono si'kuro]

It's impossible.
È impossibile.
[e impos'sibile]

Nothing of the kind (sort)!
Assolutamente no!
[assoluta'mente no!]

The exact opposite.
Esattamente il contrario!
[ezatta'mente al kon'trario!]

I'm against it.
Sono contro.
[sono 'kontro]

I don't care.
Non m'interessa.
[non minte'ressa]

I have no idea.
Non ne ho idea.
[non ne o i'dea]

I doubt it.
Dubito che sia così.
[dubito ke 'sia ko'zi]

Sorry, I can't.
Mi dispiace, non posso.
[mi dis'pjatʃe, non 'posso]

Sorry, I don't want to.
Mi dispiace, non voglio.
[mi dis'pjatʃe, non 'voʎʎo]

Thank you, but I don't need this.
Non ne ho bisogno, grazie.
[non ne o bi'zoɲo, 'gratsie]

It's getting late.
È già tardi.
[e dʒa 'tardi]

| I have to get up early. | **Devo alzarmi presto.**
[devo alts'armi 'presto] |
| I don't feel well. | **Non mi sento bene.**
[non mi 'sento 'bene] |

Expressing gratitude

Thank you.

Grazie.
[gratsie]

Thank you very much.

Grazie mille.
[gratsie 'mille]

I really appreciate it.

Le sono riconoscente.
[le 'sono rikono'ʃente]

I'm really grateful to you.

Le sono davvero grato.
[le 'sono dav'vero 'grato]

We are really grateful to you.

Le siamo davvero grati.
[le 'sjamo dav'vero 'grati]

Thank you for your time.

Grazie per la sua disponibilità.
[gratsie per la 'sua disponibili'ta]

Thanks for everything.

Grazie di tutto.
[gratsie di 'tutto]

Thank you for ...

Grazie per ...
[gratsie per ...]

your help

il suo aiuto
[il 'suo a'juto]

a nice time

il bellissimo tempo
[il bel'lissimo 'tempo]

a wonderful meal

il delizioso pranzo
[il deli'tsjozo 'prantso]

a pleasant evening

la bella serata
[la 'bella se'rata]

a wonderful day

la bella giornata
[la 'bella ʤor'nata]

an amazing journey

la splendida gita
[la 'splendida 'ʤita]

Don't mention it.

Non c'è di che.
[non ʧe di 'ke]

You are welcome.

Prego.
[prego]

Any time.

Con piacere.
[kon pja'ʧere]

My pleasure.

È stato un piacere.
[e 'stato un pja'ʧere]

Forget it.

Non ci pensi neanche.
[non ʧi 'pensi ne'aŋke]

Don't worry about it.

Non si preoccupi.
[non si pre'okkupi]

Congratulations. Best wishes

Congratulations! **Congratulazioni!**
[kongratula'tsjoni!]

Happy birthday! **Buon compleanno!**
[bu'on komple'anno!]

Merry Christmas! **Buon Natale!**
[bu'on na'tale!]

Happy New Year! **Felice Anno Nuovo!**
[fe'litʃe 'anno nu'ovo!]

Happy Easter! **Buona Pasqua!**
[bu'ona 'paskwa!]

Happy Hanukkah! **Felice Hanukkah!**
[fe'litʃe anu'ka!]

I'd like to propose a toast. **Vorrei fare un brindisi.**
[vor'rej 'fare un 'brindizi]

Cheers! **Salute!**
[sa'lute!]

Let's drink to …! **Beviamo a …!**
[be'vjamo a …!]

To our success! **Al nostro successo!**
[al 'nostro su'tʃesso!]

To your success! **Al suo successo!**
[al 'suo su'tʃesso!]

Good luck! **Buona fortuna!**
[bu'ona for'tuna!]

Have a nice day! **Buona giornata!**
[bu'ona dʒor'nata!]

Have a good holiday! **Buone vacanze!**
[bu'one va'kantse!]

Have a safe journey! **Buon viaggio!**
[bu'on 'vjadʒo!]

I hope you get better soon! **Spero guarisca presto!**
[spero gwa'riska 'presto!]

Socializing

Why are you sad?	**Perché è triste?** [per'ke e 'triste?]
Smile! Cheer up!	**Sorrida!** [sor'rida!]
Are you free tonight?	**È libero stasera?** [e 'libero sta'sera?]

May I offer you a drink?	**Posso offrirle qualcosa da bere?** [posso of'frirle kwal'koza da 'bere?]
Would you like to dance?	**Vuole ballare?** [vu'ole bal'lare?]
Let's go to the movies.	**Andiamo al cinema.** [an'djamo al 'tʃinema]

May I invite you to ...?	**Posso invitarla ...?** [posso invi'tarla ...?]
a restaurant	**al ristorante** [al risto'rante]
the movies	**al cinema** [al 'tʃinema]
the theater	**a teatro** [a te'atro]
go for a walk	**a fare una passeggiata** [per 'fare 'una passe'dʒata]

At what time?	**A che ora?** [a ke 'ora?]
tonight	**stasera** [sta'sera]
at six	**alle sei** [alle 'sei]
at seven	**alle sette** [alle 'sette]
at eight	**alle otto** [alle 'otto]
at nine	**alle nove** [alle 'nove]

Do you like it here?	**Le piace qui?** [le 'pjatʃe kwi?]
Are you here with someone?	**È qui con qualcuno?** [e kw'i kon kwal'kuno?]
I'm with my friend.	**Sono con un amico /una amica/.** [sono kon un a'miko /'una a'mika/]

I'm with my friends. **Sono con i miei amici.**
[sono kon i mjei a'mitʃi]

No, I'm alone. **No, sono da solo /sola/.**
[no, 'sono da 'solo /'sola/]

Do you have a boyfriend? **Hai il ragazzo?**
[ai il ra'gattso?]

I have a boyfriend. **Ho il ragazzo.**
[o il ra'gattso]

Do you have a girlfriend? **Hai la ragazza?**
[ai il ra'gattsa?]

I have a girlfriend. **Ho la ragazza.**
[o la ra'gattsa]

Can I see you again? **Posso rivederti?**
[posso rive'derti?]

Can I call you? **Posso chiamarti?**
[posso kja'marti?]

Call me. (Give me a call.) **Chiamami.**
['kjamami]

What's your number? **Qual'è il tuo numero?**
[kwal e il 'tuo 'numero?]

I miss you. **Mi manchi.**
[mi 'maŋki]

You have a beautiful name. **Ha un bel nome.**
[a un bel 'nome]

I love you. **Ti amo.**
[ti 'amo]

Will you marry me? **Mi vuoi sposare?**
[mi vu'oj spo'zare?]

You're kidding! **Sta scherzando!**
[sta sker'tsando!]

I'm just kidding. **Sto scherzando.**
[sto sker'tsando]

Are you serious? **Lo dice sul serio?**
[lo 'ditʃe sul 'serio?]

I'm serious. **Sono serio /seria/.**
[sono 'serio /'seria/]

Really?! **Davvero?!**
[dav'vero?!]

It's unbelievable! **È incredibile!**
[e inkre'dibile]

I don't believe you. **Non le credo.**
[non le 'kredo]

I can't. **Non posso.**
[non 'posso]

I don't know. **No so.**
[non so]

I don't understand you. **Non la capisco.**
[non la ka'pisko]

Please go away.

Per favore, vada via.
[per fa'vore, 'vada 'via]

Leave me alone!

Mi lasci in pace!
[mi 'laʃi in 'patʃe!]

I can't stand him.

Non lo sopporto.
[non lo sop'porto]

You are disgusting!

Lei è disgustoso!
[lei e dizgu'stozo!]

I'll call the police!

Chiamo la polizia!
[kjamo la poli'tsia!]

Sharing impressions. Emotions

I like it.	**Mi piace.** [mi 'pjatʃe]
Very nice.	**Molto carino.** [molto ka'rino]
That's great!	**È formidabile!** [e formi'dabile!]
It's not bad.	**Non è male.** [non e 'male]
I don't like it.	**Non mi piace.** [non mi 'pjatʃe]
It's not good.	**Questo non è buono.** [kwesto non e bu'ono]
It's bad.	**È cattivo.** [e kat'tivo]
It's very bad.	**È molto cattivo.** [e 'molto kat'tivo]
It's disgusting.	**È disgustoso.** [e dizgu'stozo]
I'm happy.	**Sono felice.** [sono fe'litʃe]
I'm content.	**Sono contento /contenta/.** [sono kon'tento /kon'tenta/]
I'm in love.	**Sono innamorato /innamorata/.** [sono innamo'rato /innamo'rata/]
I'm calm.	**Sono calmo /calma/.** [sono 'kalmo /'kalma/]
I'm bored.	**Sono annoiato /annoiata/.** [sono anno'jato /anno'jata/]
I'm tired.	**Sono stanco /stanca/.** [sono 'stanko /'stanka/]
I'm sad.	**Sono triste.** [sono 'triste]
I'm frightened.	**Sono spaventato /spaventata/.** [sono spaven'tato /spaven'tata/]
I'm angry.	**Sono arrabbiato /arrabbiata/.** [sono arrab'bjato /arrab'bjata/]
I'm worried.	**Sono preoccupato /preoccupata/.** [sono preokku'pato /preokku'pata/]
I'm nervous.	**Sono nervoso /nervosa/.** [sono ner'vozo /ner'voza/]

I'm jealous. (envious)

Sono geloso /gelosa/.
[sono ʤe'lozo /ʤe'loza/]

I'm surprised.

Sono sorpreso /sorpresa/.
[sono sor'prezo /sor'preza/]

I'm perplexed.

Sono perplesso /perplessa/.
[sono per'plesso /per'plessa/]

Problems. Accidents

I've got a problem.	**Ho un problema.** [o un pro'blema]
We've got a problem.	**Abbiamo un problema.** [ab'bjamo un pro'blema]
I'm lost.	**Sono perso /persa/.** [sono' perso /'persa/]
I missed the last bus (train).	**Ho perso l'ultimo autobus (treno).** [o 'perso 'lultimo 'autobus ('treno)]
I don't have any money left.	**Non ho più soldi.** [non o pju 'soldi]

I've lost my ...	**Ho perso ...** [o 'perso ...]
Someone stole my ...	**Mi hanno rubato ...** [mi 'anno ru'bato ...]
passport	**il passaporto** [il passa'porto]
wallet	**il portafoglio** [il porta'foʎʎo]
papers	**i documenti** [i doku'menti]
ticket	**il biglietto** [il biʎ'ʎetto]

money	**i soldi** [i 'soldi]
handbag	**la borsa** [la 'borsa]
camera	**la macchina fotografica** [la 'makkina foto'grafika]
laptop	**il computer portatile** [il kom'pjuter por'tatile]
tablet computer	**il tablet** [il 'tablet]
mobile phone	**il telefono cellulare** [il te'lefono ʧellu'lare]

Help me!	**Aiuto!** [a'juto]
What's happened?	**Che cosa è successo?** [ke 'koza e su'ʧesso?]
fire	**fuoco** [fu'oko]

shooting	**sparatoria** [spara'toria]
murder	**omicidio** [omi'tʃidio]
explosion	**esplosione** [esplo'zjone]
fight	**rissa** ['rissa]

Call the police!	**Chiamate la polizia!** [kja'mate la poli'tsia!]
Please hurry up!	**Per favore, faccia presto!** [per fa'vore, 'fatʃa 'presto!]
I'm looking for the police station.	**Sto cercando la stazione di polizia.** [sto tʃer'kando la sta'tsjone di poli'tsia]
I need to make a call.	**Devo fare una telefonata.** [devo 'fare 'una telefo'nata]
May I use your phone?	**Posso usare il suo telefono?** [posso u'zare il 'suo te'lefono?]

I've been ...	**Sono stato /stata/ ...** [sono 'stato /'stata/ ...]
mugged	**aggredito /aggredita/** [ag'gredito /ag'gredita/]
robbed	**derubato /derubata/** [deru'bato /deru'bata/]
raped	**violentata** [violen'tata]
attacked (beaten up)	**assalito /assalita/** [assa'lito /assa'lita/]

Are you all right?	**Lei sta bene?** [lei sta 'bene?]
Did you see who it was?	**Ha visto chi è stato?** [a 'visto ki e 'stato?]
Would you be able to recognize the person?	**È in grado di riconoscere la persona?** [e in 'grado di riko'noʃere la per'sona?]
Are you sure?	**È sicuro?** [e si'kuro?]

Please calm down.	**Per favore, si calmi.** [per fa'vore, si 'kalmi]
Take it easy!	**Si calmi!** [si 'kalmi!]
Don't worry!	**Non si preoccupi.** [non si pre'okkupi]
Everything will be fine.	**Andrà tutto bene.** [and'ra 'tutto 'bene]
Everything's all right.	**Va tutto bene.** [va 'tutto 'bene]
Come here, please.	**Venga qui, per favore.** [venga kwi, per fa'vore]

I have some questions for you.

Devo porle qualche domanda.
[devo 'porle 'kwalke do'manda]

Wait a moment, please.

Aspetti un momento, per favore.
[a'spetti un mo'mento, per fa'vore]

Do you have any I.D.?

Ha un documento d'identità?
[a un doku'mento didentl'ta?]

Thanks. You can leave now.

Grazie. Può andare ora.
[gratsie. pu'o an'dare 'ora]

Hands behind your head!

Mani dietro la testa!
[mani 'djetro la 'testa!]

You're under arrest!

È in arresto!
[e in ar'resto!]

Health problems

Please help me.	**Mi può aiutare, per favore.** [mi pu'o aju'tare, per fa'vore]
I don't feel well.	**Non mi sento bene.** [non mi 'sento 'bene]
My husband doesn't feel well.	**Mio marito non si sente bene.** [mio ma'rito non si 'sente 'bene]
My son ...	**Mio figlio ...** [mio 'fiʎʎo ...]
My father ...	**Mio padre ...** [mio 'padre ...]
My wife doesn't feel well.	**Mia moglie non si sente bene.** [mia 'moʎʎe non si 'sente 'bene]
My daughter ...	**Mia figlia ...** [mia 'fiʎʎa ...]
My mother ...	**Mia madre ...** [mia 'madre ...]
I've got a ...	**Ho mal di ...** [o mal di ...]
headache	**testa** [testa]
sore throat	**gola** [gola]
stomach ache	**pancia** ['pantʃa]
toothache	**denti** [denti]
I feel dizzy.	**Mi gira la testa.** [mi 'dʒira la 'testa]
He has a fever.	**Ha la febbre.** [a la 'febbre]
She has a fever.	**Ha la febbre.** [a la 'febbre]
I can't breathe.	**Non riesco a respirare.** [non ri'esko a respi'rare]
I'm short of breath.	**Mi manca il respiro.** [mi 'manka il re'spiro]
I am asthmatic.	**Sono asmatico /asmatica/.** [sono az'matiko /az'matika/]
I am diabetic.	**Sono diabetico /diabetica/.** [sono dia'betiko /dia'betika/]

I can't sleep.	**Soffro d'insonnia.** [soffro din'sonnia]
food poisoning	**intossicazione alimentare** [intossikat'tsjone alimen'tare]

It hurts here.	**Fa male qui.** [fa 'male kwi]
Help me!	**Mi aiuti!** [mi a'juti!]
I am here!	**Sono qui!** [sono kwi!]
We are here!	**Siamo qui!** [sjamo kwi!]
Get me out of here!	**Mi tiri fuori di qui!** [mi 'tiri fu'ori di kwi!]
I need a doctor.	**Ho bisogno di un dottore.** [o bi'zoɲo di un dot'tore]
I can't move.	**Non riesco a muovermi.** [non ri'esko a mu'overmi]
I can't move my legs.	**Non riesco a muovere le gambe.** [non ri'esko a mu'overe le 'gambe]

I have a wound.	**Ho una ferita.** [o 'una fe'rita]
Is it serious?	**È grave?** [e 'grave?]
My documents are in my pocket.	**I miei documenti sono in tasca.** [i 'mjei doku'menti 'sono in 'taska]
Calm down!	**Si calmi!** [si 'kalmi!]
May I use your phone?	**Posso usare il suo telefono?** [posso u'zare il 'suo te'lefono?]

Call an ambulance!	**Chiamate l'ambulanza!** [kja'mate lambu'lantsa!]
It's urgent!	**È urgente!** [e ur'dʒente!]
It's an emergency!	**È un'emergenza!** [e un emer'dʒentsa!]
Please hurry up!	**Per favore, faccia presto!** [per fa'vore, 'fatʃa 'presto!]
Would you please call a doctor?	**Per favore, chiamate un medico.** [per fa'vore, kja'mate un 'mediko]
Where is the hospital?	**Dov'è l'ospedale?** [dov'e lospe'dale?]

How are you feeling?	**Come si sente?** [kome si 'sente?]
Are you all right?	**Sta bene?** [sta 'bene?]
What's happened?	**Che cosa è successo?** [ke 'koza e su'tʃesso?]

I feel better now.

Mi sento meglio ora.
[mi 'sento 'meʎʎo 'ora]

It's OK.

Va bene.
[va 'bene]

It's all right.

Va tutto bene.
[va 'tutto 'bene]

At the pharmacy

pharmacy (drugstore)	**farmacia** [farma'tʃija]
24-hour pharmacy	**farmacia di turno** [farma'tʃija di 'turno]
Where is the closest pharmacy?	**Dov'è la farmacia più vicina?** [dov'e la farma'tʃija pju vi'tʃina?]
Is it open now?	**È aperta a quest'ora?** [e a'perta a 'kwest 'ora?]
At what time does it open?	**A che ora apre?** [a ke 'ora 'apre?]
At what time does it close?	**A che ora chiude?** [a ke 'ora 'kjude?]
Is it far?	**È lontana?** [e lon'tana?]
Can I get there on foot?	**Posso andarci a piedi?** [posso an'dartʃi a 'pjedi?]
Can you show me on the map?	**Può mostrarmi sulla piantina?** [pu'o mo'strarmi 'sulla pjan'tina?]
Please give me something for ...	**Per favore, può darmi qualcosa per ...** [per fa'vore, pu'o 'darmi kwal'koza per ...]
a headache	**il mal di testa** [il mal di 'testa]
a cough	**la tosse** [la 'tosse]
a cold	**il raffreddore** [il raffred'dore]
the flu	**l'influenza** [linflu'entsa]
a fever	**la febbre** [la 'febbre]
a stomach ache	**il mal di stomaco** [il mal di 'stomako]
nausea	**la nausea** [la 'nauzea]
diarrhea	**la diarrea** [la diar'rea]
constipation	**la costipazione** [la kostipa'tsjone]
pain in the back	**mal di schiena** [mal di 'skjena]

chest pain

dolore al petto
[do'lore al 'petto]

side stitch

fitte al fianco
[fitte al 'fjanko]

abdominal pain

dolori addominali
[do'lori addomi'nali]

pill

pastiglia
[pa'stiʎʎa]

ointment, cream

pomata
[po'mata]

syrup

sciroppo
[ʃi'roppo]

spray

spray
[spraj]

drops

gocce
[gotʃe]

You need to go to the hospital.

Deve andare in ospedale.
[deve an'dare in ospe'dale]

health insurance

assicurazione sanitaria
[assikura'tsjone sani'taria]

prescription

prescrizione
[preskri'tsjone]

insect repellant

insettifugo
[inset'tifugo]

Band Aid

cerotto
[tʃe'rotto]

The bare minimum

Excuse me, …	**Mi scusi, …** [mi 'skuzi, …]
Hello.	**Buongiorno.** [buon'dʒorno]
Thank you.	**Grazie.** [gratsie]
Good bye.	**Arrivederci.** [arrive'dertʃi]
Yes.	**Sì.** [si]
No.	**No.** [no]
I don't know.	**Non lo so.** [non lo so]
Where? | Where to? | When?	**Dove? | Dove? | Quando?** [dove? | 'dove? | 'kwando?]
I need …	**Ho bisogno di …** [o bi'zoɲo di …]
I want …	**Voglio …** [voʎʎo …]
Do you have …?	**Avete …?** [a'vete …?]
Is there a … here?	**C'è un /una/ … qui?** [tʃe un /'una/ … kwi?]
May I …?	**Posso …?** [posso …?]
…, please (polite request)	**per favore** [per fa'vore]
I'm looking for …	**Sto cercando …** [sto tʃer'kando …]
the restroom	**bagno** [baɲo]
an ATM	**bancomat** [bankomat]
a pharmacy (drugstore)	**farmacia** [farma'tʃija]
a hospital	**ospedale** [ospe'dale]
the police station	**stazione di polizia** [sta'tsjone di poli'tsia]
the subway	**metropolitana** [metropoli'tana]

a taxi	**taxi** ['taksi]
the train station	**stazione** [sta'tsjone]

My name is ...	**Mi chiamo ...** [mi 'kjamo ...]
What's your name?	**Come si chiama?** [kome si 'kjama?]
Could you please help me?	**Mi può aiutare, per favore?** [mi pu'o aju'tare, per fa'vore?]
I've got a problem.	**Ho un problema.** [o un pro'blema]
I don't feel well.	**Mi sento male.** [mi 'sento 'male]
Call an ambulance!	**Chiamate l'ambulanza!** [kja'mate lambu'lantsa!]
May I make a call?	**Posso fare una telefonata?** [posso 'fare 'una telefo'nata?]

I'm sorry.	**Mi dispiace.** [mi dis'pjatʃe]
You're welcome.	**Prego.** [prego]

I, me	**io** [io]
you (inform.)	**tu** [tu]
he	**lui** [lui]
she	**lei** ['lei]
they (masc.)	**loro** [loro]
they (fem.)	**loro** [loro]
we	**noi** [noi]
you (pl)	**voi** [voi]
you (sg, form.)	**Lei** ['lei]

ENTRANCE	**ENTRATA** [en'trata]
EXIT	**USCITA** [u'ʃita]
OUT OF ORDER	**FUORI SERVIZIO** [fu'ori ser'vitsio]
CLOSED	**CHIUSO** [kjuzo]

OPEN	**APERTO** [a'perto]
FOR WOMEN	**DONNE** [donne]
FOR MEN	**UOMINI** [u'omini]

BOOKS

T&P

CONCISE DICTIONARY

This section contains more than 1,500 useful words arranged alphabetically. The dictionary includes a lot of gastronomic terms and will be helpful when ordering food at a restaurant or buying groceries

T&P Books Publishing

DICTIONARY CONTENTS

T&P Books Publishing

T&P Books Publishing

time	**tempo** (m)	['tempo]
hour	**ora** (f)	['ora]
half an hour	**mezzora** (f)	[med'dzora]
minute	**minuto** (m)	[mi'nuto]
second	**secondo** (m)	[se'kondo]
today (adv)	**oggi**	['odʒi]
tomorrow (adv)	**domani**	[do'mani]
yesterday (adv)	**ieri**	['jeri]
Monday	**lunedì** (m)	[lune'di]
Tuesday	**martedì** (m)	[marte'di]
Wednesday	**mercoledì** (m)	[merkole'di]
Thursday	**giovedì** (m)	[dʒove'di]
Friday	**venerdì** (m)	[vener'di]
Saturday	**sabato** (m)	['sabato]
Sunday	**domenica** (f)	[do'menika]
day	**giorno** (m)	['dʒorno]
working day	**giorno** (m) **lavorativo**	['dʒorno lavora'tivo]
public holiday	**giorno** (m) **festivo**	['dʒorno fes'tivo]
weekend	**fine** (m) **settimana**	['fine setti'mana]
week	**settimana** (f)	[setti'mana]
last week (adv)	**la settimana scorsa**	[la setti'mana 'skorsa]
next week (adv)	**la settimana prossima**	[la setti'mana 'prossima]
sunrise	**levata** (f) **del sole**	[le'vata del 'sole]
sunset	**tramonto** (m)	[tra'monto]
in the morning	**di mattina**	[di mat'tina]
in the afternoon	**nel pomeriggio**	[nel pome'ridʒo]
in the evening	**di sera**	[di 'sera]
tonight (this evening)	**stasera**	[sta'sera]
at night	**di notte**	[di 'notte]
midnight	**mezzanotte** (f)	[meddza'notte]
January	**gennaio** (m)	[dʒen'najo]
February	**febbraio** (m)	[feb'brajo]
March	**marzo** (m)	['martso]
April	**aprile** (m)	[a'prile]
May	**maggio** (m)	['madʒo]
June	**giugno** (m)	['dʒuɲo]

July	luglio (m)	['luʎʎo]
August	agosto (m)	[a'gosto]
September	settembre (m)	[set'tembre]
October	ottobre (m)	[ot'tobre]
November	novembre (m)	[no'vembre]
December	dicembre (m)	[di'ʧembre]
in spring	in primavera	[in prima'vera]
in summer	in estate	[in e'state]
in fall	in autunno	[in au'tunno]
in winter	in inverno	[in in'verno]
month	mese (m)	['meze]
season (summer, etc.)	stagione (f)	[sta'dʒone]
year	anno (m)	['anno]
century	secolo (m)	['sekolo]

2. Numbers. Numerals

digit, figure	cifra (f)	['ʧifra]
number	numero (m)	['numero]
minus sign	meno (m)	['meno]
plus sign	più (m)	['pju]
sum, total	somma (f)	['somma]
first (adj)	primo	['primo]
second (adj)	secondo	[se'kondo]
third (adj)	terzo	['tertso]
0 zero	zero (m)	['dzero]
1 one	uno	['uno]
2 two	due	['due]
3 three	tre	['tre]
4 four	quattro	['kwattro]
5 five	cinque	['ʧinkwe]
6 six	sei	['sej]
7 seven	sette	['sette]
8 eight	otto	['otto]
9 nine	nove	['nove]
10 ten	dieci	['djeʧi]
11 eleven	undici	['undiʧi]
12 twelve	dodici	['dodiʧi]
13 thirteen	tredici	['trediʧi]
14 fourteen	quattordici	[kwat'tordiʧi]
15 fifteen	quindici	['kwindiʧi]
16 sixteen	sedici	['sediʧi]
17 seventeen	diciassette	[diʧas'sette]

18 eighteen	diciotto	[di'tʃotto]
19 nineteen	diciannove	[ditʃan'nove]
20 twenty	venti	['venti]
30 thirty	trenta	['trenta]
40 forty	quaranta	[kwa'ranta]
50 fifty	cinquanta	[tʃin'kwanta]
60 sixty	sessanta	[ses'santa]
70 seventy	settanta	[set'tanta]
80 eighty	ottanta	[ot'tanta]
90 ninety	novanta	[no'vanta]
100 one hundred	cento	['tʃento]
200 two hundred	duecento	[due'tʃento]
300 three hundred	trecento	[tre'tʃento]
400 four hundred	quattrocento	[kwattro'tʃento]
500 five hundred	cinquecento	[tʃinkwe'tʃento]
600 six hundred	seicento	[sej'tʃento]
700 seven hundred	settecento	[sette'tʃento]
800 eight hundred	ottocento	[otto'tʃento]
900 nine hundred	novecento	[nove'tʃento]
1000 one thousand	mille	['mille]
10000 ten thousand	diecimila	['djetʃi 'mila]
one hundred thousand	centomila	[tʃento'mila]
million	milione (m)	[mi'ljone]
billion	miliardo (m)	[mi'ljardo]

3. Humans. Family

man (adult male)	uomo (m)	[u'omo]
young man	giovane (m)	['dʒovane]
teenager	adolescente (m, f)	[adole'ʃente]
woman	donna (f)	['donna]
girl (young woman)	ragazza (f)	[ra'gattsa]
age	età (f)	[e'ta]
adult (adj)	adulto (m)	[a'dulto]
middle-aged (adj)	di mezza età	[di 'meddza e'ta]
elderly (adj)	anziano	[an'tsjano]
old (adj)	vecchio	['vekkio]
old man	vecchio (m)	['vekkio]
old woman	vecchia (f)	['vekkia]
retirement	pensionamento (m)	[pensjona'mento]
to retire (from job)	andare in pensione	[an'dare in pen'sjone]
retiree	pensionato (m)	[pensjo'nato]

mother	madre (f)	['madre]
father	padre (m)	['padre]
son	figlio (m)	['fiʎʎo]
daughter	figlia (f)	['fiʎʎa]
brother	fratello (m)	[fra'tello]
sister	sorella (f)	[so'rella]

parents	genitori (m pl)	[dʒeni'tori]
child	bambino (m)	[bam'bino]
children	bambini (m pl)	[bam'bini]
stepmother	matrigna (f)	[ma'triɲa]
stepfather	patrigno (m)	[pa'triɲo]

grandmother	nonna (f)	['nonna]
grandfather	nonno (m)	['nonno]
grandson	nipote (m)	[ni'pote]
granddaughter	nipote (f)	[ni'pote]
grandchildren	nipoti (pl)	[ni'poti]

uncle	zio (m)	['tsio]
aunt	zia (f)	['tsia]
nephew	nipote (m)	[ni'pote]
niece	nipote (f)	[ni'pote]

wife	moglie (f)	['moʎʎe]
husband	marito (m)	[ma'rito]
married (masc.)	sposato	[spo'zato]
married (fem.)	sposata	[spo'zata]
widow	vedova (f)	['vedova]
widower	vedovo (m)	['vedovo]

| name (first name) | nome (m) | ['nome] |
| surname (last name) | cognome (m) | [ko'ɲome] |

relative	parente (m)	[pa'rente]
friend (masc.)	amico (m)	[a'miko]
friendship	amicizia (f)	[ami'tʃitsia]

partner	partner (m)	['partner]
superior (n)	capo (m), superiore (m)	['kapo], [supe'rjore]
colleague	collega (m)	[kol'lega]
neighbors	vicini (m pl)	[vi'tʃini]

4. Human body

organism (body)	organismo (m)	[orga'nizmo]
body	corpo (m)	['korpo]
heart	cuore (m)	[ku'ore]
blood	sangue (m)	['sangue]
brain	cervello (m)	[tʃer'vello]

nerve	**nervo** (m)	['nervo]
bone	**osso** (m)	['osso]
skeleton	**scheletro** (m)	['skeletro]
spine (backbone)	**colonna** (f) **vertebrale**	[ko'lonna verte'brale]
rib	**costola** (f)	['kostola]
skull	**cranio** (m)	['kranio]
muscle	**muscolo** (m)	['muskolo]
lungs	**polmoni** (m pl)	[pol'moni]
skin	**pelle** (f)	['pelle]
head	**testa** (f)	['testa]
face	**viso** (m)	['vizo]
nose	**naso** (m)	['nazo]
forehead	**fronte** (f)	['fronte]
cheek	**guancia** (f)	['gwantʃa]
mouth	**bocca** (f)	['bokka]
tongue	**lingua** (f)	['lingua]
tooth	**dente** (m)	['dente]
lips	**labbra** (f pl)	['labbra]
chin	**mento** (m)	['mento]
ear	**orecchio** (m)	[o'rekkio]
neck	**collo** (m)	['kollo]
throat	**gola** (f)	['gola]
eye	**occhio** (m)	['okkio]
pupil	**pupilla** (f)	[pu'pilla]
eyebrow	**sopracciglio** (m)	[sopra'tʃiʎʎo]
eyelash	**ciglio** (m)	['tʃiʎʎo]
hair	**capelli** (m pl)	[ka'pelli]
hairstyle	**pettinatura** (f)	[pettina'tura]
mustache	**baffi** (m pl)	['baffi]
beard	**barba** (f)	['barba]
to have (a beard, etc.)	**portare** (vt)	[por'tare]
bald (adj)	**calvo**	['kalvo]
hand	**mano** (f)	['mano]
arm	**braccio** (m)	['bratʃo]
finger	**dito** (m)	['dito]
nail	**unghia** (f)	['ungia]
palm	**palmo** (m)	['palmo]
shoulder	**spalla** (f)	['spalla]
leg	**gamba** (f)	['gamba]
foot	**pianta** (f) **del piede**	['pjanta del 'pjede]
knee	**ginocchio** (m)	[dʒi'nokkio]
heel	**tallone** (m)	[tal'lone]
back	**schiena** (f)	['skjena]
waist	**vita** (f)	['vita]

beauty mark	neo (m)	['neo]
birthmark	voglia (f)	['voʎʎa]
(café au lait spot)		

5. Medicine. Diseases. Drugs

health	salute (f)	[sa'lute]
well (not sick)	sano	['sano]
sickness	malattia (f)	[malat'tia]
to be sick	essere malato	['essere ma'lato]
ill, sick (adj)	malato	[ma'lato]

cold (illness)	raffreddore (m)	[raffred'dore]
to catch a cold	raffreddarsi (vr)	[raffred'darsi]
tonsillitis	tonsillite (f)	[tonsil'lite]
pneumonia	polmonite (f)	[polmo'nite]
flu, influenza	influenza (f)	[influ'entsa]

runny nose (coryza)	raffreddore (m)	[raffred'dore]
cough	tosse (f)	['tosse]
to cough (vi)	tossire (vi)	[tos'sire]
to sneeze (vi)	starnutire (vi)	[starnu'tire]

stroke	ictus (m) cerebrale	['iktus ʧere'brale]
heart attack	attacco (m) di cuore	[at'tako di ku'ore]
allergy	allergia (f)	[aller'ʤia]
asthma	asma (f)	['azma]
diabetes	diabete (m)	[dia'bete]

tumor	tumore (m)	[tu'more]
cancer	cancro (m)	['kankro]
alcoholism	alcolismo (m)	[alko'lizmo]
AIDS	AIDS (m)	['aids]
fever	febbre (f)	['febbre]
seasickness	mal (m) di mare	[mal di 'mare]

bruise (hématome)	livido (m)	['livido]
bump (lump)	bernoccolo (m)	[ber'nokkolo]
to limp (vi)	zoppicare (vi)	[ʣoppi'kare]
dislocation	slogatura (f)	[zloga'tura]
to dislocate (vt)	slogarsi (vr)	[zlo'garsi]

fracture	frattura (f)	[frat'tura]
burn (injury)	scottatura (f)	[skotta'tura]
injury	ferita (f)	[fe'rita]
pain, ache	dolore (m), male (m)	[do'lore], ['male]
toothache	mal (m) di denti	[mal di 'denti]

| to sweat (perspire) | sudare (vi) | [su'dare] |
| deaf (adj) | sordo | ['sordo] |

mute (adj)	muto	['muto]
immunity	immunità (f)	[immuni'ta]
virus	virus (m)	['virus]
microbe	microbo (m)	['mikrobo]
bacterium	batterio (m)	[bat'terio]
infection	infezione (f)	[infe'tsjone]
hospital	ospedale (m)	[ospe'dale]
cure	cura (f)	['kura]
to vaccinate (vt)	vaccinare (vt)	[vatʃi'nare]
to be in a coma	essere in coma	['essere in 'koma]
intensive care	rianimazione (f)	[rianima'tsjone]
symptom	sintomo (m)	['sintomo]
pulse (heartbeat)	polso (m)	['polso]

6. Feelings. Emotions. Conversation

I, me	io	['io]
you	tu	['tu]
he	lui	['luj]
she	lei	['lej]
we	noi	['noj]
you (to a group)	voi	['voi]
they	loro, essi	['loro], ['essi]
Hello! (fam.)	Buongiorno!	[buon'dʒorno]
Hello! (form.)	Salve!	['salve]
Good morning!	Buongiorno!	[buon'dʒorno]
Good afternoon!	Buon pomeriggio!	[bu'on pome'ridʒo]
Good evening!	Buonasera!	[buona'sera]
to say hello	salutare (vt)	[salu'tare]
to greet (vt)	salutare (vt)	[salu'tare]
How are you?	Come va?	['kome 'va]
Bye-Bye! Goodbye!	Arrivederci!	[arrive'dertʃi]
Thank you!	Grazie!	['gratsie]
feelings	sentimenti (m pl)	[senti'menti]
to be hungry	avere fame	[a'vere 'fame]
to be thirsty	avere sete	[a'vere 'sete]
tired (adj)	stanco	['stanko]
to be worried	essere preoccupato	['essere preokku'pato]
to be nervous	essere nervoso	['essere ner'vozo]
hope	speranza (f)	[spe'rantsa]
to hope (vi, vt)	sperare (vi, vt)	[spe'rare]
character	carattere (m)	[ka'rattere]
modest (adj)	modesto	[mo'desto]

lazy (adj)	**pigro**	['pigro]
generous (adj)	**generoso**	[dʒene'rozo]
talented (adj)	**di talento**	[di ta'lento]
honest (adj)	**onesto**	[o'nesto]
serious (adj)	**serio**	['serio]
shy, timid (adj)	**timido**	['timido]
sincere (adj)	**sincero**	[sin'tʃero]
coward	**codardo** (m)	[ko'dardo]
to sleep (vi)	**dormire** (vi)	[dor'mire]
dream	**sogno** (m)	['soɲo]
bed	**letto** (m)	['letto]
pillow	**cuscino** (m)	[ku'ʃino]
insomnia	**insonnia** (f)	[in'sonnia]
to go to bed	**andare a letto**	[an'dare a 'letto]
nightmare	**incubo** (m)	['inkubo]
alarm clock	**sveglia** (f)	['zveʎʎa]
smile	**sorriso** (m)	[sor'rizo]
to smile (vi)	**sorridere** (vi)	[sor'ridere]
to laugh (vi)	**ridere** (vi)	['ridere]
quarrel	**litigio** (m)	[li'tidʒo]
insult	**insulto** (m)	[in'sulto]
resentment	**offesa** (f)	[of'feza]
angry (mad)	**arrabbiato**	[arrab'bjato]

7. Clothing. Personal accessories

clothes	**vestiti** (m pl)	[ve'stiti]
coat (overcoat)	**cappotto** (m)	[kap'potto]
fur coat	**pelliccia** (f)	[pel'litʃa]
jacket (e.g., leather ~)	**giubbotto** (m), **giaccha** (f)	[dʒub'botto], ['dʒakka]
raincoat (trenchcoat, etc.)	**impermeabile** (m)	[imperme'abile]
shirt (button shirt)	**camicia** (f)	[ka'mitʃa]
pants	**pantaloni** (m pl)	[panta'loni]
suit jacket	**giacca** (f)	['dʒakka]
suit	**abito** (m) **da uomo**	['abito da u'omo]
dress (frock)	**abito** (m)	['abito]
skirt	**gonna** (f)	['gonna]
T-shirt	**maglietta** (f)	[maʎ'ʎetta]
bathrobe	**accappatoio** (m)	[akkappa'tojo]
pajamas	**pigiama** (m)	[pi'dʒama]
workwear	**tuta** (f) **da lavoro**	['tuta da la'voro]
underwear	**intimo** (m)	['intimo]
socks	**calzini** (m pl)	[kal'tsini]

bra	reggiseno (m)	[redʒi'seno]
pantyhose	collant (m)	[kol'lant]
stockings (thigh highs)	calze (f pl)	['kaltse]
bathing suit	costume (m) da bagno	[ko'stume da 'baɲo]
hat	cappello (m)	[kap'pello]
footwear	calzature (f pl)	[kaltsa'ture]
boots (e.g., cowboy ~)	stivali (m pl)	[sti'vali]
heel	tacco (m)	['takko]
shoestring	laccio (m)	['latʃo]
shoe polish	lucido (m) per le scarpe	['lutʃido per le 'skarpe]
cotton (n)	cotone (m)	[ko'tone]
wool (n)	lana (f)	['lana]
fur (n)	pelliccia (f)	[pel'litʃa]
gloves	guanti (m pl)	['gwanti]
mittens	manopole (f pl)	[ma'nopole]
scarf (muffler)	sciarpa (f)	['ʃarpa]
glasses (eyeglasses)	occhiali (m pl)	[ok'kjali]
umbrella	ombrello (m)	[om'brello]
tie (necktie)	cravatta (f)	[kra'vatta]
handkerchief	fazzoletto (m)	[fattso'letto]
comb	pettine (m)	['pettine]
hairbrush	spazzola (f) per capelli	['spattsola per ka'pelli]
buckle	fibbia (f)	['fibbia]
belt	cintura (f)	[tʃin'tura]
purse	borsetta (f)	[bor'setta]
collar	collo (m)	['kollo]
pocket	tasca (f)	['taska]
sleeve	manica (f)	['manika]
fly (on trousers)	patta (f)	['patta]
zipper (fastener)	cerniera (f) lampo	[tʃer'njera 'lampo]
button	bottone (m)	[bot'tone]
to get dirty (vi)	sporcarsi (vr)	[spor'karsi]
stain (mark, spot)	macchia (f)	['makkia]

8. City. Urban institutions

store	negozio (m)	[ne'gotsio]
shopping mall	centro (m) commerciale	['tʃentro kommer'tʃale]
supermarket	supermercato (m)	[supermer'kato]
shoe store	negozio (m) di scarpe	[ne'gotsio di 'skarpe]
bookstore	libreria (f)	[libre'ria]
drugstore, pharmacy	farmacia (f)	[farma'tʃia]
bakery	panetteria (f)	[panette'ria]

pastry shop	**pasticceria** (f)	[pastitʃe'ria]
grocery store	**drogheria** (f)	[droge'ria]
butcher shop	**macelleria** (f)	[matʃelle'ria]
produce store	**fruttivendolo** (m)	[frutti'vendolo]
market	**mercato** (m)	[mer'kato]
hair salon	**salone** (m) **di parrucchiere**	[sa'lone di parruk'kjere]
post office	**ufficio** (m) **postale**	[uf'fitʃo po'stale]
dry cleaners	**lavanderia** (f) **a secco**	[lavande'ria a 'sekko]
circus	**circo** (m)	['tʃirko]
zoo	**zoo** (m)	['dzoo]
theater	**teatro** (m)	[te'atro]
movie theater	**cinema** (m)	['tʃinema]
museum	**museo** (m)	[mu'zeo]
library	**biblioteca** (f)	[biblio'teka]
mosque	**moschea** (f)	[mos'kea]
synagogue	**sinagoga** (f)	[sina'goga]
cathedral	**cattedrale** (f)	[katte'drale]
temple	**tempio** (m)	['tempjo]
church	**chiesa** (f)	['kjeza]
college	**istituto** (m)	[isti'tuto]
university	**università** (f)	[universi'ta]
school	**scuola** (f)	['skwola]
hotel	**albergo** (m)	[al'bergo]
bank	**banca** (f)	['banka]
embassy	**ambasciata** (f)	[amba'ʃata]
travel agency	**agenzia** (f) **di viaggi**	[adʒen'tsia di 'vjadʒi]
subway	**metropolitana** (f)	[metropoli'tana]
hospital	**ospedale** (m)	[ospe'dale]
gas station	**distributore** (m) **di benzina**	[distribu'tore di ben'dzina]
parking lot	**parcheggio** (m)	[par'kedʒo]
ENTRANCE	**ENTRATA**	[en'trata]
EXIT	**USCITA**	[u'ʃita]
PUSH	**SPINGERE**	['spindʒere]
PULL	**TIRARE**	[ti'rare]
OPEN	**APERTO**	[a'perto]
CLOSED	**CHIUSO**	['kjuzo]
monument	**monumento** (m)	[monu'mento]
fortress	**fortezza** (f)	[for'tettsa]
palace	**palazzo** (m)	[pa'lattso]
medieval (adj)	**medievale**	[medje'vale]
ancient (adj)	**antico**	[an'tiko]

| national (adj) | nazionale | [natsio'nale] |
| famous (monument, etc.) | famoso | [fa'mozo] |

9. Money. Finances

money	soldi (m pl)	['soldi]
coin	moneta (f)	[mo'neta]
dollar	dollaro (m)	['dollaro]
euro	euro (m)	['euro]

ATM	bancomat (m)	['bankomat]
currency exchange	ufficio (m) dei cambi	[uf'fitʃo dei 'kambi]
exchange rate	corso (m) di cambio	['korso di 'kambio]
cash	contanti (m pl)	[kon'tanti]

How much?	Quanto?	['kwanto]
to pay (vi, vt)	pagare (vi, vt)	[pa'gare]
payment	pagamento (m)	[paga'mento]
change (give the ~)	resto (m)	['resto]

price	prezzo (m)	['prettso]
discount	sconto (m)	['skonto]
cheap (adj)	a buon mercato	[a bu'on mer'kato]
expensive (adj)	caro	['karo]

bank	banca (f)	['banka]
account	conto (m)	['konto]
credit card	carta (f) di credito	['karta di 'kredito]
check	assegno (m)	[as'seɲo]
to write a check	emettere un assegno	[e'mettere un as'seɲo]
checkbook	libretto (m) di assegni	[li'bretto di as'seɲi]

debt	debito (m)	['debito]
debtor	debitore (m)	[debi'tore]
to lend (money)	prestare (vt)	[pre'stare]
to borrow (vi, vt)	prendere in prestito	['prendere in 'prestito]

to rent (~ a tuxedo)	noleggiare (vt)	[nole'dʒare]
on credit (adv)	a credito	[a 'kredito]
wallet	portafoglio (m)	[porta·'foʎʎo]
safe	cassaforte (f)	[kassa'forte]
inheritance	eredità (f)	[eredi'ta]
fortune (wealth)	fortuna (f)	[for'tuna]

tax	imposta (f)	[im'posta]
fine	multa (f), ammenda (f)	['multa], [am'menda]
to fine (vt)	multare (vt)	[mul'tare]

| wholesale (adj) | all'ingrosso | [all in'grosso] |
| retail (adj) | al dettaglio | [al det'taʎʎo] |

to insure (vt)	**assicurare** (vt)	[assiku'rare]
insurance	**assicurazione** (f)	[assikura'tsjone]
capital	**capitale** (m)	[kapi'tale]
turnover	**giro** (m) **di affari**	['dʒiro di af'fari]
stock (share)	**azione** (f)	[a'tsjone]
profit	**profitto** (m)	[pro'fitto]
profitable (adj)	**redditizio**	[redi'titsio]
crisis	**crisi** (f)	['krizi]
bankruptcy	**bancarotta** (f)	[banka'rotta]
to go bankrupt	**fallire** (vi)	[fal'lire]
accountant	**contabile** (m)	[kon'tabile]
salary	**stipendio** (m)	[sti'pendio]
bonus (money)	**premio** (m)	['premio]

10. Transportation

bus	**autobus** (m)	['autobus]
streetcar	**tram** (m)	[tram]
trolley bus	**filobus** (m)	['filobus]
to go by ...	**andare in ...**	[an'dare in]
to get on (~ the bus)	**salire su ...**	[sa'lire su]
to get off ...	**scendere da ...**	['ʃendere da]
stop (e.g., bus ~)	**fermata** (f)	[fer'mata]
terminus	**capolinea** (m)	[kapo'linea]
schedule	**orario** (m)	[o'rario]
ticket	**biglietto** (m)	[biʎ'ʎetto]
to be late (for ...)	**essere in ritardo**	['essere in ri'tardo]
taxi, cab	**taxi** (m)	['taksi]
by taxi	**in taxi**	[in 'taksi]
taxi stand	**parcheggio** (m) **di taxi**	[par'kedʒo di 'taksi]
traffic	**traffico** (m)	['traffiko]
rush hour	**ore** (f pl) **di punta**	['ore di 'punta]
to park (vi)	**parcheggiarsi** (vr)	[parke'dʒarsi]
subway	**metropolitana** (f)	[metropoli'tana]
station	**stazione** (f)	[sta'tsjone]
train	**treno** (m)	['treno]
train station	**stazione** (f) **ferroviaria**	[sta'tsjone ferro'vjaria]
rails	**rotaie** (f pl)	[ro'taje]
compartment	**scompartimento** (m)	[skomparti'mento]
berth	**cuccetta** (f)	[ku'tʃetta]
airplane	**aereo** (m)	[a'ereo]
air ticket	**biglietto** (m) **aereo**	[biʎ'ʎetto a'ereo]

| airline | compagnia (f) aerea | [kompa'ɲia a'erea] |
| airport | aeroporto (m) | [aero'porto] |

flight (act of flying)	volo (m)	['volo]
luggage	bagaglio (m)	[ba'gaʎʎo]
luggage cart	carrello (m)	[kar'rello]

ship	nave (f)	['nave]
cruise ship	transatlantico (m)	[transat'lantiko]
yacht	yacht (m)	[jot]
boat (flat-bottomed ~)	barca (f)	['barka]

captain	capitano (m)	[kapi'tano]
cabin	cabina (f)	[ka'bina]
port (harbor)	porto (m)	['porto]

bicycle	bicicletta (f)	[bitʃi'kletta]
scooter	motorino (m)	[moto'rino]
motorcycle, bike	motocicletta (f)	[motoʧi'kletta]
pedal	pedale (m)	[pe'dale]
pump	pompa (f)	['pompa]
wheel	ruota (f)	[ru'ota]

automobile, car	automobile (f)	[auto'mobile]
ambulance	ambulanza (f)	[ambu'lantsa]
truck	camion (m)	['kamjon]
used (adj)	di seconda mano	[di se'konda 'mano]
car crash	incidente (m)	[inʧi'dente]
repair	riparazione (f)	[ripara'tsjone]

11. Food. Part 1

meat	carne (f)	['karne]
chicken	pollo (m)	['pollo]
duck	anatra (f)	['anatra]

pork	maiale (m)	[ma'jale]
veal	vitello (m)	[vi'tello]
lamb	agnello (m)	[a'ɲello]
beef	manzo (m)	['mandzo]

sausage (bologna, etc.)	salame (m)	[sa'lame]
egg	uovo (m)	[u'ovo]
fish	pesce (m)	['peʃe]
cheese	formaggio (m)	[for'madʒo]
sugar	zucchero (m)	['dzukkero]
salt	sale (m)	['sale]

| rice | riso (m) | ['rizo] |
| pasta (macaroni) | pasta (f) | ['pasta] |

butter	burro (m)	['burro]
vegetable oil	olio (m) vegetale	['oljo vedʒe'tale]
bread	pane (m)	['pane]
chocolate (n)	cioccolato (m)	[tʃokko'lato]

wine	vino (m)	['vino]
coffee	caffè (m)	[kaf'fe]
milk	latte (m)	['latte]
juice	succo (m)	['sukko]
beer	birra (f)	['birra]
tea	tè (m)	[te]

tomato	pomodoro (m)	[pomo'doro]
cucumber	cetriolo (m)	[tʃetri'olo]
carrot	carota (f)	[ka'rota]
potato	patata (f)	[pa'tata]
onion	cipolla (f)	[tʃi'polla]
garlic	aglio (m)	['aʎʎo]

cabbage	cavolo (m)	['kavolo]
beet	barbabietola (f)	[barba'bjetola]
eggplant	melanzana (f)	[melan'tsana]
dill	aneto (m)	[a'neto]
lettuce	lattuga (f)	[lat'tuga]
corn (maize)	mais (m)	['mais]

fruit	frutto (m)	['frutto]
apple	mela (f)	['mela]
pear	pera (f)	['pera]
lemon	limone (m)	[li'mone]
orange	arancia (f)	[a'rantʃa]
strawberry (garden ~)	fragola (f)	['fragola]

plum	prugna (f)	['pruɲa]
raspberry	lampone (m)	[lam'pone]
pineapple	ananas (m)	[ana'nas]
banana	banana (f)	[ba'nana]
watermelon	anguria (f)	[an'guria]
grape	uva (f)	['uva]
melon	melone (m)	[me'lone]

12. Food. Part 2

cuisine	cucina (f)	[ku'tʃina]
recipe	ricetta (f)	[ri'tʃetta]
food	cibo (m)	['tʃibo]

to have breakfast	fare colazione	['fare kola'tsjone]
to have lunch	pranzare (vi)	[pran'tsare]
to have dinner	cenare (vi)	[tʃe'nare]

taste, flavor	gusto (m)	['gusto]
tasty (adj)	buono, gustoso	[bu'ono], [gu'stozo]
cold (adj)	freddo	['freddo]
hot (adj)	caldo	['kaldo]
sweet (sugary)	dolce	['doltʃe]
salty (adj)	salato	[sa'lato]

sandwich (bread)	panino (m)	[pa'nino]
side dish	contorno (m)	[kon'torno]
filling (for cake, pie)	ripieno (m)	[ri'pjeno]
sauce	salsa (f)	['salsa]
piece (of cake, pie)	pezzo (m)	['pettso]

diet	dieta (f)	[di'eta]
vitamin	vitamina (f)	[vita'mina]
calorie	caloria (f)	[kalo'ria]
vegetarian (n)	vegetariano (m)	[vedʒeta'rjano]

restaurant	ristorante (m)	[risto'rante]
coffee house	caffè (m)	[kaf'fe]
appetite	appetito (m)	[appe'tito]
Enjoy your meal!	Buon appetito!	[bu'on appe'tito]

waiter	cameriere (m)	[kame'rjere]
waitress	cameriera (f)	[kame'rjera]
bartender	barista (m)	[ba'rista]
menu	menù (m)	[me'nu]

spoon	cucchiaio (m)	[kuk'kjajo]
knife	coltello (m)	[kol'tello]
fork	forchetta (f)	[for'ketta]
cup (e.g., coffee ~)	tazza (f)	['tattsa]

plate (dinner ~)	piatto (m)	['pjatto]
saucer	piattino (m)	[pjat'tino]
napkin (on table)	tovagliolo (m)	[tovaʎ'ʎolo]
toothpick	stuzzicadenti (m)	[stuttsika'denti]

to order (meal)	ordinare (vt)	[ordi'nare]
course, dish	piatto (m)	['pjatto]
portion	porzione (f)	[por'tsjone]
appetizer	antipasto (m)	[anti'pasto]
salad	insalata (f)	[insa'lata]
soup	minestra (f)	[mi'nestra]

dessert	dolce (m)	['doltʃe]
jam (whole fruit jam)	marmellata (f)	[marmel'lata]
ice-cream	gelato (m)	[dʒe'lato]

check	conto (m)	['konto]
to pay the check	pagare il conto	[pa'gare il 'konto]
tip	mancia (f)	['mantʃa]

13. House. Apartment. Part 1

house	casa (f)	['kaza]
country house	casa (f) di campagna	['kaza di kam'paɲa]
villa (seaside ~)	villa (f)	['villa]

floor, story	piano (m)	['pjano]
entrance	entrata (f)	[en'trata]
wall	muro (m)	['muro]
roof	tetto (m)	['tetto]
chimney	ciminiera (f)	[ʧimi'njera]

attic (storage place)	soffitta (f)	[sof'fitta]
window	finestra (f)	[fi'nestra]
window ledge	davanzale (m)	[davan'tsale]
balcony	balcone (m)	[bal'kone]

stairs (stairway)	scala (f)	['skala]
mailbox	cassetta (f) della posta	[kas'setta 'della 'posta]
garbage can	secchio (m) della spazzatura	['sekkio 'della spattsa'tura]
elevator	ascensore (m)	[aʃen'sore]

electricity	elettricità (f)	[elettriʧi'ta]
light bulb	lampadina (f)	[lampa'dina]
switch	interruttore (m)	[interrut'tore]
wall socket	presa (f) elettrica	['preza e'lettrika]
fuse	fusibile (m)	[fu'zibile]

door	porta (f)	['porta]
handle, doorknob	maniglia (f)	[ma'niʎʎa]
key	chiave (f)	['kjave]
doormat	zerbino (m)	[ʣer'bino]

door lock	serratura (f)	[serra'tura]
doorbell	campanello (m)	[kampa'nello]
knock (at the door)	bussata (f)	[bus'sata]
to knock (vi)	bussare (vi)	[bus'sare]
peephole	spioncino (m)	[spion'ʧino]

yard	cortile (m)	[kor'tile]
garden	giardino (m)	[dʒar'dino]
swimming pool	piscina (f)	[pi'ʃina]
gym (home gym)	palestra (f)	[pa'lestra]
tennis court	campo (m) da tennis	['kampo da 'tennis]
garage	garage (m)	[ga'raʒ]

private property	proprietà (f) privata	[proprie'ta pri'vata]
warning sign	cartello (m) di avvertimento	['kartello di avverti'mento]
security	sicurezza (f)	[siku'rettsa]

security guard	**guardia** (f) **giurata**	['gwardia dʒu'rata]
renovations	**lavori** (m pl) **di restauro**	[la'vori di re'stauro]
to renovate (vt)	**rinnovare** (vt)	[rinno'vare]
to put in order	**mettere in ordine**	['mettere in 'ordine]
to paint (~ a wall)	**pitturare** (vt)	[pittu'rare]
wallpaper	**carta** (f) **da parati**	['karta da pa'rati]
to varnish (vt)	**verniciare** (vt)	[verni'tʃare]
pipe	**tubo** (m)	['tubo]
tools	**strumenti** (m pl)	[stru'menti]
basement	**seminterrato** (m)	[seminter'rato]
sewerage (system)	**fognatura** (f)	[foɲa'tura]

14. House. Apartment. Part 2

apartment	**appartamento** (m)	[apparta'mento]
room	**camera** (f), **stanza** (f)	['kamera], ['stantsa]
bedroom	**camera** (f) **da letto**	['kamera da 'letto]
dining room	**sala** (f) **da pranzo**	['sala da 'prantso]
living room	**salotto** (m)	[sa'lotto]
study (home office)	**studio** (m)	['studio]
entry room	**ingresso** (m)	[in'gresso]
bathroom (room with a bath or shower)	**bagno** (m)	['baɲo]
half bath	**gabinetto** (m)	[gabi'netto]
floor	**pavimento** (m)	[pavi'mento]
ceiling	**soffitto** (m)	[sof'fitto]
to dust (vt)	**spolverare** (vt)	[spolve'rare]
vacuum cleaner	**aspirapolvere** (m)	[aspira·'polvere]
to vacuum (vt)	**passare l'aspirapolvere**	[pas'sare laspira·'polvere]
mop	**frettazzo** (m)	[fret'tattso]
dust cloth	**strofinaccio** (m)	[strofi'natʃo]
short broom	**scopa** (f)	['skopa]
dustpan	**paletta** (f)	[pa'letta]
furniture	**mobili** (m pl)	['mobili]
table	**tavolo** (m)	['tavolo]
chair	**sedia** (f)	['sedia]
armchair	**poltrona** (f)	[pol'trona]
bookcase	**libreria** (f)	[libre'ria]
shelf	**ripiano** (m)	[ri'pjano]
wardrobe	**armadio** (m)	[ar'madio]
mirror	**specchio** (m)	['spekkio]
carpet	**tappeto** (m)	[tap'peto]

fireplace	camino (m)	[ka'mino]
drapes	tende (f pl)	['tende]
table lamp	lampada (f) da tavolo	['lampada da 'tavolo]
chandelier	lampadario (m)	[lampa'dario]
kitchen	cucina (f)	[ku'tʃina]
gas stove (range)	fornello (m) a gas	[for'nello a gas]
electric stove	fornello (m) elettrico	[for'nello e'lettriko]
microwave oven	forno (m) a microonde	['forno a mikro'onde]
refrigerator	frigorifero (m)	[frigo'rifero]
freezer	congelatore (m)	[kondʒela'tore]
dishwasher	lavastoviglie (f)	[lavasto'viʎʎe]
faucet	rubinetto (m)	[rubi'netto]
meat grinder	tritacarne (m)	[trita'karne]
juicer	spremifrutta (m)	[spremi'frutta]
toaster	tostapane (m)	[tosta'pane]
mixer	mixer (m)	['mikser]
coffee machine	macchina (f) da caffè	['makkina da kaf'fe]
kettle	bollitore (m)	[bolli'tore]
teapot	teiera (f)	[te'jera]
TV set	televisore (m)	[televi'zore]
VCR (video recorder)	videoregistratore (m)	[video·redʒistra'tore]
iron (e.g., steam ~)	ferro (m) da stiro	['ferro da 'stiro]
telephone	telefono (m)	[te'lefono]

15. Professions. Social status

director	direttore (m)	[diret'tore]
superior	capo (m), superiore (m)	['kapo], [supe'rjore]
president	presidente (m)	[prezi'dente]
assistant	assistente (m)	[assi'stente]
secretary	segretario (m)	[segre'tario]
owner, proprietor	proprietario (m)	[proprie'tario]
partner	partner (m)	['partner]
stockholder	azionista (m)	[atsio'nista]
businessman	uomo (m) d'affari	[u'omo daf'fari]
millionaire	milionario (m)	[miljo'nario]
billionaire	miliardario (m)	[miljar'dario]
actor	attore (m)	[at'tore]
architect	architetto (m)	[arki'tetto]
banker	banchiere (m)	[baŋ'kjere]
broker	broker (m)	['broker]
veterinarian	veterinario (m)	[veteri'nario]

doctor	**medico** (m)	['mediko]
chambermaid	**cameriera** (f)	[kame'rjera]
designer	**designer** (m)	[di'zajner]
correspondent	**corrispondente** (m)	[korrispon'dente]
delivery man	**fattorino** (m)	[fatto'rino]
electrician	**elettricista** (m)	[elettri'tʃista]
musician	**musicista** (m)	[muzi'tʃista]
babysitter	**baby-sitter** (f)	[bebi'siter]
hairdresser	**parrucchiere** (m)	[parruk'kjere]
herder, shepherd	**pastore** (m)	[pa'store]
singer (masc.)	**cantante** (m)	[kan'tante]
translator	**traduttore** (m)	[tradut'tore]
writer	**scrittore** (m)	[skrit'tore]
carpenter	**falegname** (m)	[fale'ɲame]
cook	**cuoco** (m)	[ku'oko]
fireman	**pompiere** (m)	[pom'pjere]
police officer	**poliziotto** (m)	[poli'tsjotto]
mailman	**postino** (m)	[po'stino]
programmer	**programmatore** (m)	[programma'tore]
salesman (store staff)	**commesso** (m)	[kom'messo]
worker	**operaio** (m)	[ope'rajo]
gardener	**giardiniere** (m)	[dʒardi'njere]
plumber	**idraulico** (m)	[i'drauliko]
dentist	**dentista** (m)	[den'tista]
flight attendant (fem.)	**hostess** (f)	['ostess]
dancer (masc.)	**danzatore** (m)	[dantsa'tore]
bodyguard	**guardia** (f) **del corpo**	['gwardia del 'korpo]
scientist	**scienziato** (m)	[ʃien'tsjato]
schoolteacher	**insegnante** (m, f)	[inse'ɲante]
farmer	**fattore** (m)	[fat'tore]
surgeon	**chirurgo** (m)	[ki'rurgo]
miner	**minatore** (m)	[mina'tore]
chef (kitchen chef)	**capocuoco** (m)	[kapo·ku'oko]
driver	**autista** (m)	[au'tista]

16. Sport

kind of sports	**sport** (m)	[sport]
soccer	**calcio** (m)	['kaltʃo]
hockey	**hockey** (m)	['okkej]
basketball	**pallacanestro** (m)	[pallaka'nestro]
baseball	**baseball** (m)	['bejzbol]
volleyball	**pallavolo** (m)	[palla'volo]
boxing	**pugilato** (m)	[pudʒi'lato]

wrestling	**lotta** (f)	['lotta]
tennis	**tennis** (m)	['tennis]
swimming	**nuoto** (m)	[nu'oto]
chess	**scacchi** (m pl)	['skakki]
running	**corsa** (f)	['korsa]
athletics	**atletica** (f) **leggera**	[a'tletika le'dʒera]
figure skating	**pattinaggio** (m) **artistico**	[patti'nadʒo ar'tistiko]
cycling	**ciclismo** (m)	[tʃik'lizmo]
billiards	**biliardo** (m)	[bi'ljardo]
bodybuilding	**culturismo** (m)	[kultu'rizmo]
golf	**golf** (m)	[golf]
scuba diving	**immersione** (f) **subacquea**	[immer'sjone su'bakvea]
sailing	**vela** (f)	['vela]
archery	**tiro** (m) **con l'arco**	['tiro kon 'larko]
period, half	**tempo** (m)	['tempo]
half-time	**intervallo** (m)	[inter'vallo]
tie	**pareggio** (m)	[pa'redʒo]
to tie (vi)	**pareggiare** (vi)	[pare'dʒare]
treadmill	**tapis roulant** (m)	[ta'pi ru'lan]
player	**giocatore** (m)	[dʒoka'tore]
substitute	**riserva** (f)	[ri'zerva]
substitutes bench	**panchina** (f)	[paŋ'kina]
match	**partita** (f)	[par'tita]
goal	**porta** (f)	['porta]
goalkeeper	**portiere** (m)	[por'tjere]
goal (score)	**gol** (m)	[gol]
Olympic Games	**Giochi** (m pl) **Olimpici**	['dʒoki o'limpitʃi]
to set a record	**stabilire un record**	[stabi'lire un 'rekord]
final	**finale** (m)	[fi'nale]
champion	**campione** (m)	[kam'pjone]
championship	**campionato** (m)	[kampjo'nato]
winner	**vincitore** (m)	[vintʃi'tore]
victory	**vittoria** (f)	[vit'toria]
to win (vi)	**vincere** (vi)	['vintʃere]
to lose (not win)	**perdere** (vt)	['perdere]
medal	**medaglia** (f)	[me'daʎʎa]
first place	**primo posto** (m)	['primo 'posto]
second place	**secondo posto** (m)	[se'kondo 'posto]
third place	**terzo posto** (m)	['tertso 'posto]
stadium	**stadio** (m)	['stadio]
fan, supporter	**tifoso, fan** (m)	[ti'fozo], [fan]
trainer, coach	**allenatore** (m)	[allena'tore]
training	**allenamento** (m)	[allena'mento]

17. Foreign languages. Orthography

language	lingua (f)	['lingua]
to study (vt)	studiare (vt)	[stu'djare]
pronunciation	pronuncia (f)	[pro'nuntʃa]
accent	accento (m)	[a'tʃento]

noun	sostantivo (m)	[sostan'tivo]
adjective	aggettivo (m)	[adʒet'tivo]
verb	verbo (m)	['verbo]
adverb	avverbio (m)	[av'verbio]

pronoun	pronome (m)	[pro'nome]
interjection	interiezione (f)	[interje'tsjone]
preposition	preposizione (f)	[prepozi'tsjone]

root	radice (f)	[ra'ditʃe]
ending	desinenza (f)	[dezi'nentsa]
prefix	prefisso (m)	[pre'fisso]
syllable	sillaba (f)	['sillaba]
suffix	suffisso (m)	[suf'fisso]

stress mark	accento (m)	[a'tʃento]
period, dot	punto (m)	['punto]
comma	virgola (f)	['virgola]
colon	due punti	['due 'punti]
ellipsis	puntini (m pl) di sospensione	[pun'tini di sospen'sjone]

question	domanda (f)	[do'manda]
question mark	punto (m) interrogativo	['punto interroga'tivo]
exclamation point	punto (m) esclamativo	['punto esklama'tivo]

in quotation marks	tra virgolette	[tra virgo'lette]
in parenthesis	tra parentesi	[tra pa'rentezi]
letter	lettera (f)	['lettera]
capital letter	lettera (f) maiuscola	['lettera ma'juskola]

sentence	proposizione (f)	[propozi'tsjone]
group of words	gruppo (m) di parole	['gruppo di pa'role]
expression	espressione (f)	[espres'sjone]

subject	soggetto (m)	[so'dʒetto]
predicate	predicato (m)	[predi'kato]
line	riga (f)	['riga]
paragraph	capoverso (m)	[kapo'verso]

synonym	sinonimo (m)	[si'nonimo]
antonym	antonimo (m)	[an'tonimo]
exception	eccezione (f)	[etʃe'tsjone]
to underline (vt)	sottolineare (vt)	[sottoline'are]

rules	**regole** (f pl)	['regole]
grammar	**grammatica** (f)	[gram'matika]
vocabulary	**lessico** (m)	['lessiko]
phonetics	**fonetica** (f)	[fo'netika]
alphabet	**alfabeto** (m)	[alfa'beto]
textbook	**manuale** (m)	[manu'ale]
dictionary	**dizionario** (m)	[ditsjo'nario]
phrasebook	**frasario** (m)	[fra'zario]
word	**vocabolo** (m)	[vo'kabolo]
meaning	**significato** (m)	[siɲifi'kato]
memory	**memoria** (f)	[me'moria]

18. The Earth. Geography

the Earth	**la Terra**	[la 'terra]
the globe (the Earth)	**globo** (m) **terrestre**	['globo ter'restre]
planet	**pianeta** (m)	[pja'neta]
geography	**geografia** (f)	[dʒeogra'fia]
nature	**natura** (f)	[na'tura]
map	**carta** (f) **geografica**	['karta dʒeo'grafika]
atlas	**atlante** (m)	[a'tlante]
in the north	**al nord**	[al nord]
in the south	**al sud**	[al sud]
in the west	**all'ovest**	[all 'ovest]
in the east	**all'est**	[all 'est]
sea	**mare** (m)	['mare]
ocean	**oceano** (m)	[o'tʃeano]
gulf (bay)	**golfo** (m)	['golfo]
straits	**stretto** (m)	['stretto]
continent (mainland)	**continente** (m)	[konti'nente]
island	**isola** (f)	['izola]
peninsula	**penisola** (f)	[pe'nizola]
archipelago	**arcipelago** (m)	[artʃi'pelago]
harbor	**porto** (m)	['porto]
coral reef	**barriera** (f) **corallina**	[bar'rjera koral'lina]
shore	**litorale** (m)	[lito'rale]
coast	**costa** (f)	['kosta]
flow (flood tide)	**alta marea** (f)	['alta ma'rea]
ebb (ebb tide)	**bassa marea** (f)	['bassa ma'rea]
latitude	**latitudine** (f)	[lati'tudine]
longitude	**longitudine** (f)	[londʒi'tudine]

parallel	**parallelo** (m)	[paral'lelo]
equator	**equatore** (m)	[ekwa'tore]
sky	**cielo** (m)	['tʃelo]
horizon	**orizzonte** (m)	[orid'dzonte]
atmosphere	**atmosfera** (f)	[atmo'sfera]
mountain	**monte** (m), **montagna** (f)	['monte], [mon'taɲa]
summit, top	**cima** (f)	['tʃima]
cliff	**falesia** (f)	[fa'lezia]
hill	**collina** (f)	[kol'lina]
volcano	**vulcano** (m)	[vul'kano]
glacier	**ghiacciaio** (m)	[gja'tʃajo]
waterfall	**cascata** (f)	[kas'kata]
plain	**pianura** (f)	[pja'nura]
river	**fiume** (m)	['fjume]
spring (natural source)	**fonte** (f)	['fonte]
bank (of river)	**riva** (f)	['riva]
downstream (adv)	**a valle**	[a 'valle]
upstream (adv)	**a monte**	[a 'monte]
lake	**lago** (m)	['lago]
dam	**diga** (f)	['diga]
canal	**canale** (m)	[ka'nale]
swamp (marshland)	**palude** (f)	[pa'lude]
ice	**ghiaccio** (m)	['gjatʃo]

19. Countries of the world. Part 1

Europe	**Europa** (f)	[eu'ropa]
European Union	**Unione** (f) **Europea**	[uni'one euro'pea]
European (n)	**europeo** (m)	[euro'peo]
European (adj)	**europeo**	[euro'peo]
Austria	**Austria** (f)	['austria]
Great Britain	**Gran Bretagna** (f)	[gran bre'taɲa]
England	**Inghilterra** (f)	[ingil'terra]
Belgium	**Belgio** (m)	['beldʒo]
Germany	**Germania** (f)	[dʒer'mania]
Netherlands	**Paesi Bassi** (m pl)	[pa'ezi 'bassi]
Holland	**Olanda** (f)	[o'landa]
Greece	**Grecia** (f)	['gretʃa]
Denmark	**Danimarca** (f)	[dani'marka]
Ireland	**Irlanda** (f)	[ir'landa]
Iceland	**Islanda** (f)	[iz'landa]
Spain	**Spagna** (f)	['spaɲa]

Italy	**Italia** (f)	[i'talia]
Cyprus	**Cipro** (m)	['tʃipro]
Malta	**Malta** (f)	['malta]

Norway	**Norvegia** (f)	[nor'vedʒa]
Portugal	**Portogallo** (f)	[porto'gallo]
Finland	**Finlandia** (f)	[fin'landia]
France	**Francia** (f)	['frantʃa]
Sweden	**Svezia** (f)	['zvetsia]

Switzerland	**Svizzera** (f)	['zvittsera]
Scotland	**Scozia** (f)	['skotsia]
Vatican	**Vaticano** (m)	[vati'kano]
Liechtenstein	**Liechtenstein** (m)	['liktenstajn]
Luxembourg	**Lussemburgo** (m)	[lussem'burgo]

Monaco	**Monaco** (m)	['monako]
Albania	**Albania** (f)	[alba'nia]
Bulgaria	**Bulgaria** (f)	[bulga'ria]
Hungary	**Ungheria** (f)	[unge'ria]
Latvia	**Lettonia** (f)	[let'tonia]

Lithuania	**Lituania** (f)	[litu'ania]
Poland	**Polonia** (f)	[po'lonia]
Romania	**Romania** (f)	[roma'nia]
Serbia	**Serbia** (f)	['serbia]
Slovakia	**Slovacchia** (f)	[zlo'vakkia]

Croatia	**Croazia** (f)	[kro'atsia]
Czech Republic	**Repubblica** (f) **Ceca**	[re'pubblika 'tʃeka]
Estonia	**Estonia** (f)	[es'tonia]
Bosnia and Herzegovina	**Bosnia-Erzegovina** (f)	['boznia-ertse'govina]
Macedonia (Republic of ~)	**Macedonia** (f)	[matʃe'donia]

Slovenia	**Slovenia** (f)	[zlo'venia]
Montenegro	**Montenegro** (m)	[monte'negro]
Belarus	**Bielorussia** (f)	[bjelo'russia]
Moldova, Moldavia	**Moldavia** (f)	[mol'davia]
Russia	**Russia** (f)	['russia]
Ukraine	**Ucraina** (f)	[uk'raina]

20. Countries of the world. Part 2

Asia	**Asia** (f)	['azia]
Vietnam	**Vietnam** (m)	['vjetnam]
India	**India** (f)	['india]
Israel	**Israele** (m)	[izra'ele]
China	**Cina** (f)	['tʃina]
Lebanon	**Libano** (m)	['libano]
Mongolia	**Mongolia** (f)	[mo'ngolia]

Malaysia	**Malesia** (f)	[ma'lezia]
Pakistan	**Pakistan** (m)	['pakistan]
Saudi Arabia	**Arabia Saudita** (f)	[a'rabia sau'dita]

Thailand	**Tailandia** (f)	[taj'landia]
Taiwan	**Taiwan** (m)	[taj'van]
Turkey	**Turchia** (f)	[tur'kia]
Japan	**Giappone** (m)	[dʒap'pone]
Afghanistan	**Afghanistan** (m)	[af'ganistan]

Bangladesh	**Bangladesh** (m)	['bangladeʃ]
Indonesia	**Indonesia** (f)	[indo'nezia]
Jordan	**Giordania** (f)	[dʒor'dania]
Iraq	**Iraq** (m)	['irak]
Iran	**Iran** (m)	['iran]

Cambodia	**Cambogia** (f)	[kam'bodʒa]
Kuwait	**Kuwait** (m)	[ku'vejt]
Laos	**Laos** (m)	['laos]
Myanmar	**Birmania** (f)	[bir'mania]
Nepal	**Nepal** (m)	[ne'pal]

United Arab Emirates	**Emirati** (m pl) **Arabi**	[emi'rati 'arabi]
Syria	**Siria** (f)	['siria]
Palestine	**Palestina** (f)	[pale'stina]
South Korea	**Corea** (f) **del Sud**	[ko'rea del sud]
North Korea	**Corea** (f) **del Nord**	[ko'rea del nord]

United States of America	**Stati** (m pl) **Uniti d'America**	['stati u'niti da'merika]
Canada	**Canada** (m)	['kanada]
Mexico	**Messico** (m)	['messiko]
Argentina	**Argentina** (f)	[ardʒen'tina]
Brazil	**Brasile** (m)	[bra'zile]

Colombia	**Colombia** (f)	[ko'lombia]
Cuba	**Cuba** (f)	['kuba]
Chile	**Cile** (m)	['tʃile]
Venezuela	**Venezuela** (f)	[venetsu'ela]
Ecuador	**Ecuador** (m)	[ekva'dor]

The Bahamas	**le Bahamas**	[le ba'amas]
Panama	**Panama** (m)	['panama]
Egypt	**Egitto** (m)	[e'dʒitto]
Morocco	**Marocco** (m)	[ma'rokko]
Tunisia	**Tunisia** (f)	[tuni'zia]

Kenya	**Kenya** (m)	['kenia]
Libya	**Libia** (f)	['libia]
South Africa	**Repubblica** (f) **Sudafricana**	[re'pubblika sudafri'kana]
Australia	**Australia** (f)	[au'stralia]
New Zealand	**Nuova Zelanda** (f)	[nu'ova dze'landa]

21. Weather. Natural disasters

weather	tempo (m)	['tempo]
weather forecast	previsione (f) del tempo	[previ'zjone del 'tempo]
temperature	temperatura (f)	[tempera'tura]
thermometer	termometro (m)	[ter'mometro]
barometer	barometro (m)	[ba'rometro]

sun	sole (m)	['sole]
to shine (vi)	splendere (vi)	['splendere]
sunny (day)	di sole	[di 'sole]
to come up (vi)	levarsi (vr)	[le'varsi]
to set (vi)	tramontare (vi)	[tramon'tare]

rain	pioggia (f)	['pjodʒa]
it's raining	piove	['pjove]
pouring rain	pioggia (f) torrenziale	['pjodʒa torren'tsjale]
rain cloud	nube (f) di pioggia	['nube di 'pjodʒa]
puddle	pozzanghera (f)	[pot'tsangera]
to get wet (in rain)	bagnarsi (vr)	[ba'ɲarsi]

thunderstorm	temporale (m)	[tempo'rale]
lightning (~ strike)	fulmine (f)	['fulmine]
to flash (vi)	lampeggiare (vi)	[lampe'dʒare]
thunder	tuono (m)	[tu'ono]
it's thundering	tuona	[tu'ona]
hail	grandine (f)	['grandine]
it's hailing	grandina	['grandina]

heat (extreme ~)	caldo (m), afa (f)	['kaldo], ['afa]
it's hot	fa molto caldo	[fa 'molto 'kaldo]
it's warm	fa caldo	[fa 'kaldo]
it's cold	fa freddo	[fa 'freddo]

fog (mist)	foschia (f), nebbia (f)	[fos'kia], ['nebbia]
foggy	nebbioso	[neb'bjozo]
cloud	nuvola (f)	['nuvola]
cloudy (adj)	nuvoloso	[nuvo'lozo]
humidity	umidità (f)	[umidi'ta]

snow	neve (f)	['neve]
it's snowing	nevica	['nevika]
frost (severe ~, freezing cold)	gelo (m)	['dʒelo]
below zero (adv)	sotto zero	['sotto 'dzero]
hoarfrost	brina (f)	['brina]

bad weather	maltempo (m)	[mal'tempo]
disaster	disastro (m)	[di'zastro]
flood, inundation	inondazione (f)	[inonda'tsjone]
avalanche	valanga (f)	[va'langa]

earthquake	terremoto (m)	[terre'moto]
tremor, shoke	scossa (f)	['skossa]
epicenter	epicentro (m)	[epi'tʃentro]
eruption	eruzione (f)	[eru'tsjone]
lava	lava (f)	['lava]
tornado	tornado (m)	[tor'nado]
twister	tromba (f) d'aria	['tromba 'daria]
hurricane	uragano (m)	[ura'gano]
tsunami	tsunami (m)	[tsu'nami]
cyclone	ciclone (m)	[tʃi'klone]

22. Animals. Part 1

animal	animale (m)	[ani'male]
predator	predatore (m)	[preda'tore]
tiger	tigre (f)	['tigre]
lion	leone (m)	[le'one]
wolf	lupo (m)	['lupo]
fox	volpe (m)	['volpe]
jaguar	giaguaro (m)	[dʒa'gwaro]
lynx	lince (f)	['lintʃe]
coyote	coyote (m)	[ko'jote]
jackal	sciacallo (m)	[ʃa'kallo]
hyena	iena (f)	['jena]
squirrel	scoiattolo (m)	[sko'jattolo]
hedgehog	riccio (m)	['ritʃo]
rabbit	coniglio (m)	[ko'niʎʎo]
raccoon	procione (f)	[pro'tʃone]
hamster	criceto (m)	[kri'tʃeto]
mole	talpa (f)	['talpa]
mouse	topo (m)	['topo]
rat	ratto (m)	['ratto]
bat	pipistrello (m)	[pipi'strello]
beaver	castoro (m)	[kas'toro]
horse	cavallo (m)	[ka'vallo]
deer	cervo (m)	['tʃervo]
camel	cammello (m)	[kam'mello]
zebra	zebra (f)	['dzebra]
whale	balena (f)	[ba'lena]
seal	foca (f)	['foka]
walrus	tricheco (m)	[tri'keko]
dolphin	delfino (m)	[del'fino]
bear	orso (m)	['orso]

monkey	**scimmia** (f)	['ʃimmia]
elephant	**elefante** (m)	[ele'fante]
rhinoceros	**rinoceronte** (m)	[rinotʃe'ronte]
giraffe	**giraffa** (f)	[dʒi'raffa]
hippopotamus	**ippopotamo** (m)	[ippo'potamo]
kangaroo	**canguro** (m)	[kan'guro]
cat	**gatta** (f)	['gatta]
dog	**cane** (m)	['kane]
cow	**mucca** (f)	['mukka]
bull	**toro** (m)	['toro]
sheep (ewe)	**pecora** (f)	['pekora]
goat	**capra** (f)	['kapra]
donkey	**asino** (m)	['azino]
pig, hog	**porco** (m)	['porko]
hen (chicken)	**gallina** (f)	[gal'lina]
rooster	**gallo** (m)	['gallo]
duck	**anatra** (f)	['anatra]
goose	**oca** (f)	['oka]
turkey (hen)	**tacchina** (f)	[tak'kina]
sheepdog	**cane** (m) **da pastore**	['kane da pas'tore]

23. Animals. Part 2

bird	**uccello** (m)	[u'tʃello]
pigeon	**colombo** (m), **piccione** (m)	[kolombo], [pi'tʃone]
sparrow	**passero** (m)	['passero]
tit (great tit)	**cincia** (f)	['tʃintʃa]
magpie	**gazza** (f)	['gattsa]
eagle	**aquila** (f)	['akwila]
hawk	**astore** (m)	[a'store]
falcon	**falco** (m)	['falko]
swan	**cigno** (m)	['tʃiɲo]
crane	**gru** (f)	[gru]
stork	**cicogna** (f)	[tʃi'koɲa]
parrot	**pappagallo** (m)	[pappa'gallo]
peacock	**pavone** (m)	[pa'vone]
ostrich	**struzzo** (m)	['struttso]
heron	**airone** (m)	[ai'rone]
nightingale	**usignolo** (m)	[uzi'ɲolo]
swallow	**rondine** (f)	['rondine]
woodpecker	**picchio** (m)	['pikkio]
cuckoo	**cuculo** (m)	['kukulo]

owl	**civetta** (f)	[tʃi'vetta]
penguin	**pinguino** (m)	[pin'gwino]
tuna	**tonno** (m)	['tonno]
trout	**trota** (f)	['trota]
eel	**anguilla** (f)	[an'gwilla]
shark	**squalo** (m)	['skwalo]
crab	**granchio** (m)	['graŋkio]
jellyfish	**medusa** (f)	[me'duza]
octopus	**polpo** (m)	['polpo]
starfish	**stella** (f) **marina**	['stella ma'rina]
sea urchin	**riccio** (m) **di mare**	['ritʃo di 'mare]
seahorse	**cavalluccio** (m) **marino**	[kaval'lutʃo ma'rino]
shrimp	**gamberetto** (m)	[gambe'retto]
snake	**serpente** (m)	[ser'pente]
viper	**vipera** (f)	['vipera]
lizard	**lucertola** (f)	[lu'tʃertola]
iguana	**iguana** (f)	[i'gwana]
chameleon	**camaleonte** (m)	[kamale'onte]
scorpion	**scorpione** (m)	[skor'pjone]
turtle	**tartaruga** (f)	[tarta'ruga]
frog	**rana** (f)	['rana]
crocodile	**coccodrillo** (m)	[kokko'drillo]
insect, bug	**insetto** (m)	[in'setto]
butterfly	**farfalla** (f)	[far'falla]
ant	**formica** (f)	[for'mika]
fly	**mosca** (f)	['moska]
mosquito	**zanzara** (f)	[dzan'dzara]
beetle	**scarabeo** (m)	[skara'beo]
bee	**ape** (f)	['ape]
spider	**ragno** (m)	['raɲo]

24. Trees. Plants

tree	**albero** (m)	['albero]
birch	**betulla** (f)	[be'tulla]
oak	**quercia** (f)	['kwertʃa]
linden tree	**tiglio** (m)	['tiʎʎo]
aspen	**pioppo** (m) **tremolo**	['pjoppo 'tremolo]
maple	**acero** (m)	['atʃero]
spruce	**abete** (m)	[a'bete]
pine	**pino** (m)	['pino]
cedar	**cedro** (m)	['tʃedro]
poplar	**pioppo** (m)	['pjoppo]

rowan	**sorbo** (m)	['sorbo]
beech	**faggio** (m)	['fadʒo]
elm	**olmo** (m)	['olmo]
ash (tree)	**frassino** (m)	['frassino]
chestnut	**castagno** (m)	[ka'staɲo]
palm tree	**palma** (f)	['palma]
bush	**cespuglio** (m)	[ʧes'puʎʎo]
mushroom	**fungo** (m)	['fungo]
poisonous mushroom	**fungo** (m) **velenoso**	['fungo vele'nozo]
cep (Boletus edulis)	**porcino** (m)	[por'ʧino]
russula	**rossola** (f)	['rossola]
fly agaric	**ovolaccio** (m)	[ovo'laʧo]
death cap	**fungo** (m) **moscario**	['fungo mos'kario]
flower	**fiore** (m)	['fjore]
bouquet (of flowers)	**mazzo** (m) **di fiori**	['mattso di 'fjori]
rose (flower)	**rosa** (f)	['roza]
tulip	**tulipano** (m)	[tuli'pano]
carnation	**garofano** (m)	[ga'rofano]
camomile	**camomilla** (f)	[kamo'milla]
cactus	**cactus** (m)	['kaktus]
lily of the valley	**mughetto** (m)	[mu'getto]
snowdrop	**bucaneve** (m)	[buka'neve]
water lily	**ninfea** (f)	[nin'fea]
conservatory (greenhouse)	**serra** (f)	['serra]
lawn	**prato** (m) **erboso**	['prato er'bozo]
flowerbed	**aiuola** (f)	[aju'ola]
plant	**pianta** (f)	['pjanta]
grass	**erba** (f)	['erba]
leaf	**foglia** (f)	['foʎʎa]
petal	**petalo** (m)	['petalo]
stem	**stelo** (m)	['stelo]
young plant (shoot)	**germoglio** (m)	[dʒer'moʎʎo]
cereal crops	**cereali** (m pl)	[ʧere'ali]
wheat	**frumento** (m)	[fru'mento]
rye	**segale** (f)	['segale]
oats	**avena** (f)	[a'vena]
millet	**miglio** (m)	['miʎʎo]
barley	**orzo** (m)	['ortso]
corn	**mais** (m)	['mais]
rice	**riso** (m)	['rizo]

25. Various useful words

balance (of situation)	**bilancio** (m)	[bi'lantʃo]
base (basis)	**base** (f)	['baze]
beginning	**inizio** (m)	[i'nitsio]
category	**categoria** (f)	[katego'ria]
choice	**scelta** (f)	['ʃelta]
coincidence	**coincidenza** (f)	[kojntʃi'dentsa]
comparison	**confronto** (m)	[kon'fronto]
degree (extent, amount)	**grado** (m)	['grado]
development	**sviluppo** (m)	[zvi'luppo]
difference	**differenza** (f)	[diffe'rentsa]
effect (e.g., of drugs)	**effetto** (m)	[ef'fetto]
effort (exertion)	**sforzo** (m)	['sfortso]
element	**elemento** (m)	[ele'mento]
example (illustration)	**esempio** (m)	[e'zempjo]
fact	**fatto** (m)	['fatto]
help	**aiuto** (m)	[a'juto]
ideal	**ideale** (m)	[ide'ale]
kind (sort, type)	**genere** (m)	['dʒenere]
mistake, error	**errore** (m)	[er'rore]
moment	**momento** (m)	[mo'mento]
obstacle	**ostacolo** (m)	[os'takolo]
part (~ of sth)	**parte** (f)	['parte]
pause (break)	**pausa** (f)	['pauza]
position	**posizione** (f)	[pozi'tsjone]
problem	**problema** (m)	[pro'blema]
process	**processo** (m)	[pro'tʃesso]
progress	**progresso** (m)	[pro'gresso]
property (quality)	**proprietà** (f)	[proprie'ta]
reaction	**reazione** (f)	[rea'tsjone]
risk	**rischio** (m)	['riskio]
secret	**segreto** (m)	[se'greto]
series	**serie** (f)	['serie]
shape (outer form)	**forma** (f)	['forma]
situation	**situazione** (f)	[situa'tsjone]
solution	**soluzione** (f)	[solu'tsjone]
standard (adj)	**standard**	['standar]
stop (pause)	**pausa** (f)	['pauza]
style	**stile** (m)	['stile]
system	**sistema** (m)	[si'stema]

table (chart)	**tabella** (f)	[ta'bella]
tempo, rate	**ritmo** (m)	['ritmo]
term (word, expression)	**termine** (m)	['termine]
truth (e.g., moment of ~)	**verità** (f)	[veri'ta]
turn (please wait your ~)	**turno** (m)	['turno]
urgent (adj)	**urgente**	[ur'dʒente]
utility (usefulness)	**utilità** (f)	[utili'ta]
variant (alternative)	**variante** (f)	[vari'ante]
way (means, method)	**modo** (m)	['modo]
zone	**zona** (f)	['dzona]

26. Modifiers. Adjectives. Part 1

additional (adj)	**supplementare**	[supplemen'tare]
ancient (~ civilization)	**antico**	[an'tiko]
artificial (adj)	**artificiale**	[artifi'tʃale]
bad (adj)	**cattivo**	[kat'tivo]
beautiful (person)	**bello**	['bello]
big (in size)	**grande**	['grande]
bitter (taste)	**amaro**	[a'maro]
blind (sightless)	**cieco**	['tʃeko]
central (adj)	**centrale**	[tʃen'trale]
children's (adj)	**per bambini**	[per bam'bini]
clandestine (secret)	**clandestino**	[klande'stino]
clean (free from dirt)	**pulito**	[pu'lito]
clever (smart)	**intelligente**	[intelli'dʒente]
compatible (adj)	**compatibile**	[kompa'tibile]
contented (satisfied)	**contento**	[kon'tento]
dangerous (adj)	**pericoloso**	[periko'lozo]
dead (not alive)	**morto**	['morto]
dense (fog, smoke)	**denso**	['denso]
difficult (decision)	**difficile**	[dif'fitʃile]
dirty (not clean)	**sporco**	['sporko]
easy (not difficult)	**facile**	['fatʃile]
empty (glass, room)	**vuoto**	[vu'oto]
exact (amount)	**preciso**	[pre'tʃizo]
excellent (adj)	**eccellente**	[etʃel'lente]
excessive (adj)	**eccessivo**	[etʃes'sivo]
exterior (adj)	**esterno**	[e'sterno]
fast (quick)	**veloce, rapido**	[velotʃe], ['rapido]
fertile (land, soil)	**fertile**	['fertile]
fragile (china, glass)	**fragile**	['fradʒile]
free (at no cost)	**gratuito**	[gratu'ito]

fresh (~ water)	dolce	['doltʃe]
frozen (food)	surgelato	[surdʒe'lato]
full (completely filled)	pieno	['pjeno]
happy (adj)	felice	[fe'litʃe]
hard (not soft)	duro	['duro]
huge (adj)	enorme	[e'norme]
ill (sick, unwell)	malato	[ma'lato]
immobile (adj)	immobile	[im'mobile]
important (adj)	importante	[impor'tante]
interior (adj)	interno	[in'terno]
last (e.g., ~ week)	scorso	['skorso]
last (final)	ultimo	['ultimo]
left (e.g., ~ side)	sinistro	[si'nistro]
legal (legitimate)	legale	[le'gale]
light (in weight)	leggero	[le'dʒero]
liquid (fluid)	liquido	['likwido]
long (e.g., ~ hair)	lungo	['lungo]
loud (voice, etc.)	alto, forte	['alto], ['forte]
low (voice)	basso	['basso]

27. Modifiers. Adjectives. Part 2

main (principal)	principale	[printʃi'pale]
matt, matte	opaco	[o'pako]
mysterious (adj)	misterioso	[miste'rjozo]
narrow (street, etc.)	stretto	['stretto]
native (~ country)	nativo	[na'tivo]
negative (~ response)	negativo	[nega'tivo]
new (adj)	nuovo	[nu'ovo]
next (e.g., ~ week)	successivo	[sutʃes'sivo]
normal (adj)	normale	[nor'male]
not difficult (adj)	non difficile	[non dif'fitʃile]
obligatory (adj)	obbligatorio	[obbliga'torio]
old (house)	vecchio	['vekkio]
open (adj)	aperto	[a'perto]
opposite (adj)	opposto	[op'posto]
ordinary (usual)	comune, normale	[ko'mune], [nor'male]
original (unusual)	originale	[oridʒi'nale]
personal (adj)	personale	[perso'nale]
polite (adj)	gentile	[dʒen'tile]
poor (not rich)	povero	['povero]
possible (adj)	possibile	[pos'sibile]
principal (main)	principale	[printʃi'pale]

probable (adj)	probabile	[pro'babile]
prolonged (e.g., ~ applause)	continuo	[kon'tinuo]
public (open to all)	pubblico	['pubbliko]
rare (adj)	raro	['raro]
raw (uncooked)	crudo	['krudo]
right (not left)	destro	['destro]
ripe (fruit)	maturo	[ma'turo]
risky (adj)	rischioso	[ris'kjozo]
sad (~ look)	triste	['triste]
second hand (adj)	di seconda mano	[di se'konda 'mano]
shallow (water)	poco profondo	['poko pro'fondo]
sharp (blade, etc.)	affilato	[affi'lato]
short (in length)	corto	['korto]
similar (adj)	simile	['simile]
small (in size)	piccolo	['pikkolo]
smooth (surface)	liscio	['liʃo]
soft (~ toys)	morbido	['morbido]
solid (~ wall)	solido	['solido]
sour (flavor, taste)	acido, agro	['atʃido], ['agro]
spacious (house, etc.)	spazioso	[spa'tsjozo]
special (adj)	speciale	[spe'tʃale]
straight (line, road)	dritto	['dritto]
strong (person)	forte	['forte]
stupid (foolish)	stupido	['stupido]
superb, perfect (adj)	perfetto	[per'fetto]
sweet (sugary)	dolce	['doltʃe]
tan (adj)	abbronzato	[abbron'dzato]
tasty (delicious)	buono, gustoso	[bu'ono], [gu'stozo]
unclear (adj)	poco chiaro	['poko 'kjaro]

28. Verbs. Part 1

to accuse (vt)	accusare (vt)	[akku'zare]
to agree (say yes)	essere d'accordo	['essere dak'kordo]
to announce (vt)	annunciare (vt)	[annun'tʃare]
to answer (vi, vt)	rispondere (vi, vt)	[ris'pondere]
to apologize (vi)	scusarsi (vr)	[sku'zarsi]
to arrive (vi)	arrivare (vi)	[arri'vare]
to ask (~ oneself)	chiedere, domandare	['kjedere], [doman'dare]
to be absent	essere assente	['essere as'sente]
to be afraid	avere paura	[a'vere pa'ura]
to be born	nascere (vi)	['naʃere]

to be in a hurry	avere fretta	[a'vere 'fretta]
to beat (to hit)	picchiare (vt)	[pik'kjare]
to begin (vt)	cominciare (vt)	[komin'tʃare]
to believe (in God)	credere (vi)	['kredere]
to belong to ...	appartenere (vi)	[apparte'nere]
to break (split into pieces)	rompere (vt)	['rompere]
to build (vt)	costruire (vt)	[kostru'ire]
to buy (purchase)	comprare (vt)	[kom'prare]
can (v aux)	potere (v aus)	[po'tere]
can (v aux)	potere (vi)	[po'tere]
to cancel (call off)	annullare (vt)	[annul'lare]
to catch (vt)	afferrare (vt)	[affer'rare]
to change (vt)	cambiare (vt)	[kam'bjare]
to check (to examine)	verificare (vt)	[verifi'kare]
to choose (select)	scegliere (vt)	['ʃeʎʎere]
to clean up (tidy)	fare le pulizie	['fare le puli'tsie]
to close (vt)	chiudere (vt)	['kjudere]
to compare (vt)	comparare (vt)	[kompa'rare]
to complain (vi, vt)	lamentarsi (vr)	[lamen'tarsi]
to confirm (vt)	confermare (vt)	[konfer'mare]
to congratulate (vt)	congratularsi (vr)	[kongratu'larsi]
to cook (dinner)	cucinare (vi)	[kutʃi'nare]
to copy (vt)	copiare (vt)	[ko'pjare]
to cost (vt)	costare (vt)	[ko'stare]
to count (add up)	contare (vt)	[kon'tare]
to count on ...	contare su ...	[kon'tare su]
to create (vt)	creare (vt)	[kre'are]
to cry (weep)	piangere (vi)	['pjandʒere]
to dance (vi, vt)	ballare (vi, vt)	[bal'lare]
to deceive (vi, vt)	ingannare (vt)	[ingan'nare]
to decide (~ to do sth)	decidere (vt)	[de'tʃidere]
to delete (vt)	eliminare (vt)	[elimi'nare]
to demand (request firmly)	esigere (vt)	[e'zidʒere]
to deny (vt)	negare (vt)	[ne'gare]
to depend on ...	dipendere da ...	[di'pendere da]
to despise (vt)	disprezzare (vt)	[dispret'tsare]
to die (vi)	morire (vi)	[mo'rire]
to dig (vt)	scavare (vt)	[ska'vare]
to disappear (vi)	scomparire (vi)	[skompa'rire]
to discuss (vt)	discutere (vt)	[di'skutere]
to disturb (vt)	disturbare (vt)	[distur'bare]

29. Verbs. Part 2

to dive (vi)	tuffarsi (vr)	[tuf'farsi]
to divorce (vi)	divorziare (vi)	[divor'tsjare]
to do (vt)	fare (vt)	['fare]
to doubt (have doubts)	dubitare (vi)	[dubi'tare]
to drink (vi, vt)	bere (vi, vt)	['bere]
to drop (let fall)	lasciar cadere	[la'ʃar ka'dere]
to dry (clothes, hair)	asciugare (vt)	[aʃu'gare]
to eat (vi, vt)	mangiare (vi, vt)	[man'dʒare]
to end (~ a relationship)	porre fine a ...	['porre 'fine a]
to excuse (forgive)	scusare (vt)	[sku'zare]
to exist (vi)	esistere (vi)	[e'zistere]
to expect (foresee)	prevedere (vt)	[preve'dere]
to explain (vt)	spiegare (vt)	[spje'gare]
to fall (vi)	cadere (vi)	[ka'dere]
to fight (street fight, etc.)	picchiarsi (vr)	[pik'kjarsi]
to find (vt)	trovare (vt)	[tro'vare]
to finish (vt)	finire (vt)	[fi'nire]
to fly (vi)	volare (vi)	[vo'lare]
to forbid (vt)	vietare (vt)	[vje'tare]
to forget (vi, vt)	dimenticare (vt)	[dimenti'kare]
to forgive (vt)	perdonare (vt)	[perdo'nare]
to get tired	stancarsi (vr)	[stan'karsi]
to give (vt)	dare (vt)	['dare]
to go (on foot)	andare (vi)	[an'dare]
to hate (vt)	odiare (vt)	[odi'are]
to have (vt)	avere (vt)	[a'vere]
to have breakfast	fare colazione	['fare kola'tsjone]
to have dinner	cenare (vi)	[tʃe'nare]
to have lunch	pranzare (vi)	[pran'tsare]
to hear (vt)	sentire (vt)	[sen'tire]
to help (vt)	aiutare (vt)	[aju'tare]
to hide (vt)	nascondere (vt)	[na'skondere]
to hope (vi, vt)	sperare (vi, vt)	[spe'rare]
to hunt (vi, vt)	cacciare (vt)	[ka'tʃare]
to hurry (vi)	avere fretta	[a'vere 'fretta]
to insist (vi, vt)	insistere (vi)	[in'sistere]
to insult (vt)	insultare (vt)	[insul'tare]
to invite (vt)	invitare (vt)	[invi'tare]
to joke (vi)	scherzare (vi)	[sker'tsare]
to keep (vt)	conservare (vt)	[konser'vare]
to kill (vt)	uccidere (vt)	[u'tʃidere]
to know (sb)	conoscere	[ko'noʃere]

to know (sth)	sapere (vt)	[sa'pere]
to like (I like …)	piacere (vi)	[pja'tʃere]
to look at …	guardare (vt)	[gwar'dare]
to lose (umbrella, etc.)	perdere (vt)	['perdere]
to love (sb)	amare qn	[a'mare]
to make a mistake	sbagliare (vi)	[zbaʎ'ʎare]
to meet (vi, vt)	incontrarsi (vr)	[inkon'trarsi]
to miss (school, etc.)	mancare le lezioni	[man'kare le le'tsjoni]

30. Verbs. Part 3

to obey (vi, vt)	obbedire (vi)	[obbe'dire]
to open (vt)	aprire (vt)	[a'prire]
to participate (vi)	partecipare (vi)	[partetʃi'pare]
to pay (vi, vt)	pagare (vi, vt)	[pa'gare]
to permit (vt)	permettere (vt)	[per'mettere]
to play (children)	giocare (vi)	[dʒo'kare]
to pray (vi, vt)	pregare (vi, vt)	[pre'gare]
to promise (vt)	promettere (vt)	[pro'mettere]
to propose (vt)	proporre (vt)	[pro'porre]
to prove (vt)	provare (vt)	[pro'vare]
to read (vi, vt)	leggere (vi, vt)	['ledʒere]
to receive (vt)	ricevere (vt)	[ri'tʃevere]
to rent (sth from sb)	affittare (vt)	[affit'tare]
to repeat (say again)	ripetere (vt)	[ri'petere]
to reserve, to book	riservare (vt)	[rizer'vare]
to run (vi)	correre (vi)	['korrere]
to save (rescue)	salvare (vt)	[sal'vare]
to say (~ thank you)	dire (vt)	['dire]
to see (vt)	vedere (vt)	[ve'dere]
to sell (vt)	vendere (vt)	['vendere]
to send (vt)	mandare (vt)	[man'dare]
to shoot (vi)	sparare (vi)	[spa'rare]
to shout (vi)	gridare (vi)	[gri'dare]
to show (vt)	mostrare (vt)	[mo'strare]
to sign (document)	firmare (vt)	[fir'mare]
to sing (vi)	cantare (vi)	[kan'tare]
to sit down (vi)	sedersi (vr)	[se'dersi]
to smile (vi)	sorridere (vi)	[sor'ridere]
to speak (vi, vt)	parlare (vi, vt)	[par'lare]
to steal (money, etc.)	rubare (vt)	[ru'bare]
to stop (please ~ calling me)	cessare (vt)	[tʃes'sare]
to study (vt)	studiare (vt)	[stu'djare]

to swim (vi)	**nuotare** (vi)	[nuo'tare]
to take (vt)	**prendere** (vt)	['prendere]
to talk to …	**parlare con …**	[par'lare kon]
to tell (story, joke)	**raccontare** (vt)	[rakkon'tare]
to thank (vt)	**ringraziare** (vt)	[ringra'tsjare]
to think (vi, vt)	**pensare** (vi, vt)	[pen'sare]
to translate (vt)	**tradurre** (vt)	[tra'durre]
to trust (vt)	**fidarsi** (vr)	[fi'darsi]
to try (attempt)	**tentare** (vt)	[ten'tare]
to turn (e.g., ~ left)	**girare** (vi)	[dʒi'rare]
to turn off	**spegnere** (vt)	['speɲere]
to turn on	**accendere** (vt)	[a'tʃendere]
to understand (vt)	**capire** (vt)	[ka'pire]
to wait (vt)	**aspettare** (vt)	[aspet'tare]
to want (wish, desire)	**volere** (vt)	[vo'lere]
to work (vi)	**lavorare** (vi)	[lavo'rare]
to write (vt)	**scrivere** (vt)	['skrivere]

www.ingramcontent.com/pod-product-compliance
Lightning Source LLC
Chambersburg PA
CBHW060025050426
42448CB00012B/2872